The Nature of Theological Argument:
A Study of Paul Tillich

HARVARD THEOLOGICAL REVIEW
HARVARD DISSERTATIONS IN RELIGION

edited by

Caroline Bynum

and

George Rupp

Number 4

THE NATURE OF THEOLOGICAL ARGUMENT: A STUDY OF PAUL TILLICH

by

Robert William Schrader

SCHOLARS PRESS
Missoula, Montana

THE NATURE OF THEOLOGICAL ARGUMENT:

A STUDY OF PAUL TILLICH

by

Robert William Schrader

Published by

SCHOLARS PRESS

for

Harvard Theological Review

Distributed by

SCHOLARS PRESS
University of Montana
Missoula, Montana 59801

THE NATURE OF THEOLOGICAL ARGUMENT: A STUDY OF PAUL TILLICH

by

Robert William Schrader
Suomen Yogaopisto, Saarijarvi, Finland

Library of Congress Cataloging in Publication Data

Schrader, Robert William.
    The nature of theological argument.

    (Harvard dissertations in religion ; no. 4)
    Bibliography: p.
    1. Tillich, Paul, 1886-1965.   I.   Title.
II.   Series.
BX4827.T53S34   230'.092'4   75-43784
ISBN 0-89130-071-6

PRINTED IN THE UNITED STATES OF AMERICA

1 2 3 4 5
Edwards Brothers, Inc.
Ann Arbor, Michigan 48104

TABLE OF CONTENTS

TO BEVERLY, KAREN, AND ROBIN

INTRODUCTION

What is theology, and what is its function? There is a tendency among theologians today to define theology in remarkably
diverse ways, but there is also a tendency to agree that the
function of theology is to serve the church. And yet it is often
difficult to see just how a theologian's particular definition of
theology relates to his affirmation that theology serves the
church. Most theologians seem to be saying that theology has a
very practical function, and yet in practice it is seldom clear
just what value theological doctrines and debates have. If a
theologian defines theology as rational thought about faith, we
might ask what is valuable about such rational thought. Is the
life of a Christian endangered if he believes irrational things?
Or is the church interested in rational thought because it is
interested in abstract truth about God? And whatever one's
answers to the question of the value of rationality, how does one
account for the seeming failure of rational thought to gain general agreement? How does one justify continuing to do theology
if religious and doctrinal conflicts remain as deep (at least)
as they were before the time of theologians?

These questions could be multiplied indefinitely. But all
are reducible to the simple query: why should anyone do theology?
One could put this more intensely and even ask: what _right_ has
anyone to do theology, given the rather horrifying state of the
world and the multitude of seemingly more useful tasks to which
one might devote his time and energy. Surely such a question
has arisen in the mind of many theologians, especially, for example, after participating in an exhausting and often futile debate
on intricate theological questions.

Of the many ways of attempting to gain insight into such
questions, I have chosen to analyze the answers given, explicitly
and implicitly, by a prominent contemporary theologian, Paul
Tillich. Since for Tillich theology is, in part, defined as
rational thought about the Christian faith,[1] and since for him

---

[1]_Systematic Theology_ (Chicago: University of Chicago Press,
1951-1963), I, pp. 15-16, 53-59; II, p. 108; III, p. 422.
(Henceforth abbreviated _S.T._)

theology must serve the church,[2] I wish to discover in what way such rational thought serves the church. Tillich is especially interesting because he not only attempts to be rational, as we all do in some measure, but he attempts to be rational to the very highest degree: that is, he thinks philosophically or onto-logically. Perhaps most people who have dipped into his works have found themselves asking themselves, at least now and then, not only whether his abstract ontological views are true, but what they mean, and eventually even what difference it all makes.

In attempting to discover Tillich's answers to the question of what difference his theology, or any theology, makes, I intend to focus on two things: his explicit methodological remarks on the aim and criteria of theological assertions, and his actual use of these (and perhaps other) criteria in his arguments for or against particular theological assertions. Both these foci are necessary, since the former are, while often helpful and suggestive, just as often utterly confusing, and furthermore there is no obvious reason for supposing Tillich may not have imperfectly analyzed or ambiguously stated his method. In parti-cular, he often says nothing about precisely those questions which seem most pressing, and this forces us to see what clues he may offer in his actual arguments.

The kinds of arguments Tillich uses are many. He appeals to Scripture and tradition; he accuses a given doctrine of absurdity, of inconsistency, of having bad consequences, or of lacking power; and he often offers various abstract, philosophical arguments. For example, to support his claim that God is not a particular being, he argues that this view is opposed by certain parts of Scripture and tradition, that it is absurd and even a contradic-tion-in-terms, that it leads to dishonesty, that it has apologe-tic weaknesses, and that it makes God finite by splitting his essence from his existence.

What I wish to discover is what such arguments are supposed to prove, and particularly how they relate to theology's aim of serving the church. What is Tillich trying to prove when he claims that the belief in God as a highest being is dangerous? Is it necessarily dangerous, so that any theologian who asserts that God is a being is doing harm to the personal welfare, here or hereafter, of individual Christians? And what is wrong with absurdity--or for that matter with inconsistency? Is the faith or life of a believer endangered if he believes that God lives

---

[2] S.T., I, p. 3; III, pp. 201-204.

in a place far above the clouds and at the same time lives inside our souls? And if they are not endangered, then why should one do theology and claim not only that such beliefs are false but that one is serving the church by pointing out or proving that they are false?

The material for this study will be drawn mainly from Tillich's later works. Since his writings are often more expository than argumentative, I have found especially useful, at times, those works in which he finds himself forced to argue the most, such as certain "dialogical" books consisting of Tillich's responses to questions and criticisms. But once one's eyes are trained, so to speak, to discern Tillichian arguments, they can be found, however concisely and cryptically stated, throughout his works. Thus many arguments have been plucked from writings which seem at first glance to be irritatingly free of reasons.

As for Tillich's explicit methodological remarks, I have been able to make comparatively little use of the best-known ones contained, for example, in his various essays on theology and philosophy and his Introduction to the Systematic Theology. This may be my fault or Tillich's; at any rate, I have often found them too vague and general to be useful. For example, it is difficult to find any concrete criteria in his famed method of correlation. How the method of correlation functions to determine whether or not God is a being is not obvious, and I rather doubt that Tillich meant it as a statement of clear criteria. I have made much more use of Tillich's out-of-the-way comments on his method; in the midst of a particular piece of exposition or argument Tillich will sometimes reflect upon what he is doing and produce a pearl of clarity and insight.

There are three concepts around which I have organized this study, each of them designating a particular kind or level of rational thought about fiath. The three are dogma (or doctrine), system, and ontology. Thus our questions to Tillich become: why is it necessary or valuable to create dogma, to accept the systematic form (i.e., to systematize dogmas), and to incorporate ontology into one's dogma? These are enormous questions: they ultimately reduce to the question why one should do theology at all.

But we should take special note of the fact that such questions become especially urgent in a theology such as Tillich's, in which there is a resolute refusal to see faith as a matter of believing that something is true.[3] Rather, faith is described as a state of being ultimately concerned,[4] and revelation, the basis of faith, is not the revelation of "information" about this world or the next but a "being grasped" in an ecstatic experience.[5] Given such a non-intellectualist understanding of faith, what possible reason could there be to think about or conceptualize the content of faith, and indeed, what could it even mean to conceptualize it? No doubt one has the knowledge that the so-called revelatory experience or event has occurred,[6] perhaps even that one's way of life is somehow dependent upon it, but what else does one know? Why is it a pressing, or even an interesting, or even a meaningful question to ask what one knows? How do dogma, system, and ontology serve the church?

To find Tillich's answers to these questions would take us very deeply into his thought and especially into his whole way of thinking. But getting fully involved in his thought often means getting confused, and thus I propose to begin as slowly as possible. That is, I would like to begin with Tillich's simplest and clearest answers to the above questions and proceed rather cautiously to the more obscure ones. In this way we will have at least gained some clarity, however muddied the waters eventually become.

---

[3]_Dynamics_ _of_ _Faith_ (New York: Harper and Brothers, 1957), p. 31.

[4]_Ibid._, p. 1.

[5]_S.T._, I, pp. 124, 129, 157-159.

[6]_Ibid._, p. 109.

CHAPTER ONE
ONTOLOGY: ITS APOLOGETIC VALUE

Many of Tillich's remarks about the nature and aim of theology leave unanswered exactly those questions in which we are most
interested. Theology, he claims, is the _logos_ of _theos_; it involves a rational interpretation of religious symbols, myths, and
rituals.[1] Systematic theology tries to show the _rationality_ of
the Christian message.[2] The function of theology is to elaborate
"the conceptual implications of religious certainties."[3] "Theologians must make explicit what is implicit in religious thought and
expression;"[4] theology "should not weaken the concrete symbols but
it must analyze them in abstract ontological terms;"[5] theology
must transform the potential ontology of the religious language
found, for example, in the Bible, into an _actual_ ontology.[6]

The question we wish to ask of all these statements is simply, "Why so?" Why must theology be rational; why must it elaborate the conceptual implications of religious certainties; why
must it use ontology? To say, as Tillich sometimes does, that
theology must do these things because otherwise it would have to
abdicate or get rid of itself[7] is simply to beg the question, for
why _shouldn't_ theology abdicate? How do all these activities of
the theologian actually serve the church?

I think it would be fair to say that most theologians would
see little wrong in Tillich's belief that theology must be _ration-
al_--at least in _some_ sense of the word. What is more commonly
objected to in Tillich's thought is his use of a particularly
sophisticated and abstract kind of rationality, namely, ontology.
Although I believe that the question "Why rationality" is at
least as important as, and also prior to, the question "Why onto-

---

[1]_S.T._, I, pp. 15-16.

[2]_S.T._, II, p. 108.

[3]_S.T._, III, p. 422.

[4]_S.T._, I, p. 239.

[5]_Ibid._, p. 242.

[6]_S.T._, II, p. 12.

[7]_S.T._, II, p. 142.

1

logy," I would nevertheless admit that Tillich's attempt to onto-
logize somehow seems more puzzling than his mere attempt to be
rational. It is difficult enough even to figure out what his ontological language means, let alone how the use of such language
serves the church. Thus it may be instructive to begin our analysis by seeing whether Tillich suggests any clear answer at all to
the question of how an ontological theology can be useful and
even necessary.

One of the strangest things about Tillich's use of ontology
in his theology is his view that all language about God is symbolic[8] and that man cannot know God as he is in himself.[9] For one
would think that when Tillich offers a re-interpretation, in ontological terms, of a traditional Christian myth or doctrine, he is
somehow expressing more truthfully or literally the nature of God.
But for Tillich, even ontological concepts become symbolic when
used of God. That God created the world and that God is the
ground of being are both symbolic assertions. What, one might ask,
has been gained by substituting one set of symbols for another?

Tillich sometimes offers a remarkably clear answer. He gives
an _apologetic_ reason for using ontological language. If one
wishes to communicate with certain people, namely, the intellectuals, one must use their language, and ontological or philosophical concepts form part of their language. Such language "speaks"
to them; it enables them to hear the Christian message while
other kinds of language may be offensive or entirely unintelligible to them. Tillich holds that the Christian faith can be expressed in many ways. All these ways are symbolic ways of speaking, there are any number of kinds of symbols which can express
faith, and thus it is just a matter of finding the most suitable
symbols, or the most "intelligible" ones, for the people one is
trying to reach. One uses the language of one's listeners to
express what one is trying to say. In Tillich's case, the listeners he especially had in mind were the educated men, the "rational" men, the men who had a particular need for or interest in
rationality or rational language, and Tillich simply wanted to
communicate with them.

To make a rash but at this point plausible comparison, it
is almost as if Tillich were saying: nobody has ever denied that
the Christian faith can be expressed in Greek, Latin, German, and

---

[8] _S.T._, I, p. 239. Tillich here excepts the statement that
God is being-itself. But cf. _S.T._, II, pp. 9-10, where Tillich
seems to say that it is _both_ symbolic and non-symbolic.

[9] Sidney and Beatrice Rome (eds.), _Philosophical Interroga-
tions_ (New York: Holt, Rinehart and Winston, 1964), p. 378.

English; why then can it not be expressed in the "language" of
the intellectuals, a language which instead of "God" prefers
"Being-itself," instead of "sin" prefers "estrangement," and instead of "the Fall of man" prefers "the transition from essence to
existence." The intellectuals Tillich has in mind are those who
understand such terminology, and thus a theology which uses it is
both legitimate and necessary.

Tillich often gives such an interpretation of the value and
indeed point not only of his theology but of theology in general.
In the Introduction to Volume III of his Systematic Theology, he
says:

> A special characteristic of these three volumes,
> much noticed and often criticized, is the kind of
> language used in them and the way in which it is
> used. It deviates from the ordinary use of bibli-
> cal language in systematic theology--that is, to
> support particular assertions with appropriate bib-
> lical quotations. . . .Instead, philosophical and
> psychological concepts are preferred, and references
> to sociological and scientific theories often appear.
> This procedure seems more suitable for a systematic
> theology which tries to speak understandably to the
> large group of educated people, including open-
> minded students of theology, for whom traditional
> language has become irrelevant. . . .Certainly, these
> three books would not have been written if I had not
> been convinced that the event in which Christianity
> was born has central significance for all mankind,
> both before and after the event. But the way in
> which this event can be understood and received
> changes with changing conditions in all periods of
> history. . . . Since the split between a faith
> unacceptable to culture and a culture unacceptable
> to faith was not possible for me, the only alterna-
> tive was to attempt to interpret the symbols of faith
> through expressions of our own culture. The result
> of this attempt is the three volumes of Systematic
> Theology.[10] (italics mine)

One can wonder, of course, whether ontological language of the
type Tillich uses is as much a part of the vocabulary of the
intellectuals as he thinks. To this Tillich could respond by
simply pointing, for example, to the large sale of his books,
admitting that language drawn from other traditions might reach
those intellectuals who react negatively to his terminology.
Tillich might say that no theologian can speak to all intellectuals.[11] The point of all this is that there is simply no sug-

---

[10] S.T., III, pp. 4-5.

[11] Cf. Theology of Culture, ed. Robert C. Kimball (London:
Oxford University Press, 1959), p. 204: "None of us is asked to
speak to everybody in all places and periods;" and also S.T., III,
p. 203; where Tillich says that "a theology is always possible
on the basis of any philosophical tradition." He adds that even
materialism could be used.

gestion in the above passage that the "true" meaning of the
Christian faith is expressible only through the use of ontological terms like "being" or "essence" or psychological terms like
"estrangement" or "acceptance." There is not even the suggestion that it can in general be better expressed in such terms.
Tillich is only saying that such terms can be used to express
the message, and that they should be used under certain condi-
tions--i.e., when trying to speak "understandably" to certain
people "for whom traditional language has become irrelevant."
One would see little sense in speaking the Christian message in
German to a group of Eskimos; why then feel constrained to speak
in traditional language to modern men?

Of course, the comparison of different languages, such as
Greek and English, with the terminologies of different "conceptual systems," such as the traditional and the contemporary, or
the naive and the sophisticated, must not be pushed too far, but
I think Tillich's words here allow and even invite the analogy,
for he speaks as if the issue rests on questions of language,
not of truth or validity or value in some absolute sense. Further, there are grounds for giving special importance to these
remarks because they appear in the third and last volume of the
Systematic Theology, after Tillich has already attempted to justify the use of ontology in previous volumes. That is, we might
reasonably guess that Tillich is aware, because of many criticisms, that he had not been entirely clear or convincing as to
exactly why he used abstract philosophical terms, and here he
wishes decisively to set matters straight. Such language, he
seems to say, is not more adequate in some absolutistic way; it
is adequate only relatively, that is, relative to those theologians who wish to speak to certain educated men.

Indeed, Tillich has already stated much the same point,
more briefly, in the Preface to Volume II:

> Here I want to say a word to the prospective cri-
> tics of this volume. I hope to receive much valu-
> able criticism of the substance of my thought, as
> I did with the first volume and my smaller books
> . . . . But I cannot accept criticism as valuable
> which merely insinuates that I have surrendered
> the substance of the Christian message because I
> have used a terminology which consciously deviates
> from the biblical or ecclesiastical language.
> Without such deviation, I would not have deemed
> it worthwhile to develop a theological system for
> our period.[12]   (italics mine)

---

[12] S.T., II, pp. vii-viii.

Again the emphasis is on terminology for our period, and
again there is no mention at all of the greater truth expressible in ontological language or of the greater accessibility to
the truth of the intellectuals, even the Christian intellectuals.
It is very much as if the whole problem of giving rational or philosophical adequacy to the Christian faith is a matter of expressing the faith in such a way that those who are called "rational
men" or "educated men" or "philosophers" can understand it.
There is no suggestion that their understanding of faith is better than anybody else's. It makes sense to them, as the German
language makes sense to the Germans, and there need be no question of whether one of the many possible languages or ways of
thinking is intrinsically better than others.

That Tillich's special concern was not with all men of our
period but with the intellectual in particular is a point he
often makes. He states it most unequivocally, comparing himself
in an interesting way to Barth, in a discussion with students
recorded in Ultimate Concern. He states that his special task
is to speak to those who have been left alone by theologians
like Barth. "Karl Barth spoke in a very particular situation to
a very particular group of people. He spoke to those who, in
themselves, were attached to the church and who stood, as theologians or laymen, on the boundary line of a liberalism which
might finally have led to so-called Germanic Christianity. And
he saved Christianity from this pitfall."[13] But there was a
group of people to whom Barth did not speak. "The so-called
intelligentsia--the people who cannot escape the sad destiny of
having to think--was left alone."[14] Many of them have simply
rejected Christianity and all other religions. These are the
people to whom Tillich wishes to communicate the Christian message. "And I have to speak to them. My work is with those who
ask questions, and for them I am here."[15]

If we interpret these remarks in relation to Tillich's previous statements about theology being a matter of finding the
appropriate terminology, the whole dispute between Tillich and

---

[13] D. Mackenzie Brown (ed.), Ultimate Concern: Tillich in
Dialogue (New York: Harper and Row, 1965), p. 189.

[14] Ibid., p. 190.

[15] Ibid., p. 191. Cf. also pp. 88-89, where Tillich offers
"a small confession" about his work: "my whole theological work
has been directed precisely to the interpretation of religious
symbols in such a way that the secular man . . . can understand
and be moved by them."

Barth seems to approach dissolution. Tillich suggests that he
and Barth gave different solutions to the problems of theology
simply because they were speaking to different people--Barth to
"those attached to the church" (in which case a heavy dependence
on Biblical and traditional language would obviously be most
effective), and Tillich to the more or less secularized intelligentsia (for whom traditional language is unintelligible and new
forms of language are necessary). Tillich's extreme charity
toward Barth here makes one wonder what theological debate is all
about. He seems to suggest that he and Barth--and most other
theologians--differ not in essentials but in modes of expression.
"But if we try to think of this whole thing as waves on a river
we simply try to determine what we can do--what Barth did in his
way, what I do in my way, and what Bultmann and Reinhold Niebuhr
have done."[16] Perhaps, then, different theologies arise because
of different audiences. Theology has changed over the last twenty
centuries because men have changed, and at any particular time
there are various kinds of theology because there are various
kinds of men to whom the Christian message must be communicated.

If this is so, we might expect Tillich not only to use new
terminology but also to reflect carefully upon his choice of
terminology. This is indeed what he does. Most of his works
are marked by very careful attention to the question of the
appropriateness of various new and traditional terms. Indeed,
I believe that it could be maintained that he argues almost as
much about words as about doctrines. He not only offers arguments for or against particular assertions, but he also, with
remarkable frequency, offers arguments for or against the use of
particular terms. For example, he not only argues that, according to Christianity, man is sinful, but he also offers arguments
regarding whether the word "sin" is today the best word to
express the original idea.[17] He not only argues that there is
an element of ecstasy in revelation, but also that "ecstasy"
is a better term than "enthusiasm."[18] He not only forwards
arguments regarding the actuality and possibility of miracles,
but also argues that the word "miracle" itself has so many bad
connotations that another term may have to be found.[19] In general, it could be said that Tillich's examination of a given

---

[16]Ibid., pp. 192-193.

[17]S.T., II, p. 46.

[18]S.T., I, p. 112.

[19]S.T., I, p. 115.

doctrine or theological assertion is nearly always supplemented
by an examination of the appropriateness of the terms, new and
old, used to express the doctrine.[20]

When Tillich argues for or against the use of a given term,
he uses a variety of arguments. Does he ever explicitly argue
for or against a term because of its acceptability or offensive-
ness to the intellectuals? We might expect him at least to dis-
guise such arguments a bit; it might be, shall we say, counter-
productive to claim that the term "Logos" is better than "Word
of God" mainly because one's listeners prefer it. For one's
listeners are precisely those who think that philosophical language is somehow more adequate than ordinary language, and perhaps the theologian, simply to reach them, must work not against
but through these pretensions.

And yet there are times when Tillich does appear to let the
cat out of the bag. For example, in discussing why he uses the
term "ecstasy," despite the bad connotations it has acquired for
those within the church, he says: "'Ecstasy' has a legitimate
use in theology, especially in apologetic theology."[21] He does
not clarify this assertion, but perhaps a little reflection can
indicate not only what he means but also why he does not perform
the task of clarification himself. For why should the term
"ecstasy" be useful in apologetic theology? What apologetic
function could it have? One answer would be that it is a term
which would be attractive to those educated people (especially,
perhaps, the young) who have been alienated from Christianity by
its emphasis upon morality and belief and its corresponding de-
emphasis upon feeling, especially powerful feeling. These people
are often attracted to those philosophical positions, such as
some varieties of existentialism, which emphasize passion over
reason (or the Dionysian over the Apollonian), and which make
use of terms such as "ecstasy." And yet for Tillich to have
made too plain that he was using the term "ecstasy," rather than
more traditional terms, in order to reach such people might have
the effect of seeming "insincere" to the cultured. This is not
to say that Tillich really is insincere; the point is that whe-

---

[20]For only a few of the other places where Tillich gives
careful and extensive attention to reasons for and against the
use of certain terms, cf. his discussions of "justification by
faith," S.T., II, pp. 85, 179; "Word of God," S.T., I, pp. 122-
123, 157-159; "spirit," S.T., III, pp. 21-25; "inner word," S.T.,
I, pp. 125-126, III, pp. 126-127. His point is usually that
certain terms lend themselves to a particular kind of distortion,
while others more adequately protect against such distortion.

[21]S.T., I, p. 112.

ther we use the more contemporary term "ecstasy" or the more traditional term "inspiration," our terms are ultimately inadequate and distorted, and the question becomes not so much whether a certain term is really best but whether a certain term best opens certain people to the Christian message. Theology, one might say, has a profoundly rhetorical character.

Much the same comments may apply in considering Tillich's rather surprising statement, in support of his concept of God, that "many apologetic weaknesses could be avoided if God were understood first of all as being-itself or as the ground of being," rather than as the highest being.[22] Precisely why does the idea of God as the ground of being have more apologetic value than the idea of God as a being? We need only remember that the term "ground of being" (or terms like it) has become, through the efforts of various existentialist, idealist, and mystical thinkers, a rather attractive term for many of the educated, in order to understand what Tillich may be getting at. If some people simply cannot, for whatever reason, bring themselves to take seriously one who speaks of a highest being called God, perhaps they will take seriously one who speaks of God as the ground of being. God is not literally the highest being, nor is he literally the ground of being, but the second term, for some, more adequately "points" to a reality than the other.

This may clarify Tillich's odd characterization of many of his terms as "conceptual symbols." The terms "Logos" and "essentialization" are conceptual symbols;[23] the term "ground of being," he says is "partly conceptual and partly symbolical."[24] But what is this half-way house between a concept and a symbol? How can a concept be a symbol? Isn't the whole point of theology to use concepts in order to interpret symbols? What Tillich may be saying is that concepts, though not in themselves symbols any more than anything else, can (and must) become symbols if applied to God, and they are particularly useful symbols when communicating with those who find abstract concepts to have particular meaning and significance.

Tillich's discussion of the terms "estrangement" and "sin" seem to corroborate this. He says that "estrangement" as a philosophical term was created by Hegel and used even by his

---

[22] S.T., I, p. 235.

[23] S.T., II, pp. 111-112; III, p. 407.

[24] S.T., III, p. 293.

opponents, such as Marx.[25] It is "a conceptualization of the
Pauline idea that in the sin of Adam everybody has sinned."[26]
But again we might ask what the purpose of such conceptualization is. Tillich's answer seems to be that "estrangement" points
to the same reality as the term "sin" originally did, but that
today it is more easily understood by certain people.

> Now take the term "estrangement." When I speak
> in any college about estrangement everybody
> knows what I mean, because they all feel estranged
> from their true being, from life, from themselves
> especially. But if I spoke of their all being
> sinners, they would not understand at all. They
> would think "I haven't sinned; I haven't drunk or
> danced," as in some fundamentalist churches or
> whatever they understand as sin. But estrangement
> is a reality for them. Yet estrangement is what
> sin means--the power of estrangement from God.
> And that is all it means.[27]

Thus it seems as if Tillich is not trying to claim that man
is really estranged rather than sinful, or that God's revelation
occurs through ecstasy rather than inspiration, or that God is
really the ground of being rather than the highest being. He is
merely claiming that all such ways of speaking can be adequate
or inadequate depending upon to whom one is speaking, and that
an apologetic theology directed to certain intellectuals of
today will use the words best suited to the task.

Tillich's discussion of the apologetic value of the term
"acceptance" over the traditional term "justification" follows
much the same lines.[28] Of course, "acceptance" could hardly be
called a philosophical or ontological term; rather, it is probably what Tillich would call a contemporary psychological term.
But in his discussion of it he makes the interesting point that
Paul himself used the term "justification" not because of its
intrinsic adequacy but because of its _apologetic_ adequacy: he
was speaking to Jews and had no other choice but to bend Jewish
legalistic language to his purpose of preaching the Christian
message.[29] We can note that the fact that Paul himself was a
Jew and thus felt at home with legalistic language is comparable
to the fact that Tillich, like his intended hearers, is an intellectual and obviously feels at home with philosophical language.

---

[25]_S.T._, II, pp. 45.

[26]Rome, p. 400.

[27]Brown, p. 98.

[28]_S.T._, III, pp. 224-225.

[29]Ibid., p. 224.

But such biographical considerations are not strictly relevant to the question of the intended theological _reasons_ for using a particular language or way of speaking. Our point is only that, according to Tillich, what is at stake in formulating the Christian message is not eternal truth or "information" about God but the communication of something (presumably a state of being) which can be expressed in any number of ways.

I daresay that Tillich comes remarkably close in all this to identifying theology with preaching.[30] The philosophical theologian is he who, by his intellectualist bent, is particularly suited to speak to other intellectuals. He speaks their language and answers their questions much as a pastor does in dealing with his flock, or as a missionary does in dealing with his listeners. "Apostle to the intellectual," Tillich has been called,[31] and we must see how much, or how little, is entailed in that expression.

As a little experiment in thought, let us draw out the implications of this view of apologetic theology. By the same token a theologian might see his special task as speaking to the Navajo Indians instead of to the educated, alienated intellectuals. He might then wish to point to parallels and analogies between Navajo and Christian symbols. He would try to use their terminology and their concepts as part of the situation, in terms of which he must express himself; at the same time he would be careful not to become so preoccupied in the task of expressing himself in Navajo ideas that he distorted the Christian message. And if one asks what makes him think it is possible to use Navajo language and concepts to express without distortion the Christian message, the answer is that, first, _no_ words can express the message without _any_ distortion, and further, that the Christian's confidence that the Christian message has central significance for all mankind means the message must be _expressible_ to all men—and obviously in their own terminology.

Again, suppose the theologian were trying to speak especially to lawyers and judges; he might emphasize the various traditional concepts which are particularly intelligible and significant to such people—terms like justice, law, forgiveness, etc. On the other hand, in speaking to farmers the theologian might use as symbolic material the notions which are fraught

---

[30] Or, perhaps better, with _missionary_ activity, which is directed more toward those outside than toward those inside the church.

[31] Brown, p. 193.

with special significance for people who live from the land, such
as those relating to the seasons and the weather. In each of
these cases a theology might be developed which paralleled Tillich's in many respects, except instead of giving the philosophical or theoretical "transformation"[32] of a type of faith (in this
case, the Christian faith), one would develop its Navajo or legalistic or agricultural transformation. The point, after all, is
only to speak meaningfully to these different people in the language closest to their hearts.

At this point, however, we begin to suspect that we have
gone awry. What we seem to have done above is to characterize
various kinds of preaching, perhaps, but surely theology is somehow to be distinguished from preaching. Does not Tillich in
some sense wish to say that the term "power of being" is more
adequate than the term "creator?" Can one avoid the idea that
Tillich sees philosophical language as more than a mere apologetic tool? For surely he would not claim that the statement,
"God is the ground of our being" is merely an apologetic statement which happens to speak to the intellectual as the statement
"God is the source of the weather" might speak to the farmer.
We cannot avoid getting into the question of the relation between
theology and ontology quite that easily, as if it would be
enough to show that in fact ontological language, for whatever
reason, is successful in opening the Christian message to a certain group and is therefore necessary in a certain kind of apologetic theology. We cannot explain and justify his use of ontological language by merely pointing to the large sale of his
books, his immense classes at Harvard, or the fact that he was
respected by many of the intelligentsia.

For we must note, to begin with, that Tillich would surely
not give the name "theology" to all transformations or transla-
tions of the Christian message. Indeed, he seems to link apologetic theology in general, and not simply his own apologetic
theology, to philosophy. His description of the contrast between
philosophical and kerygmatic theology in an address on philosophy and theology[33] is nearly identical with his later description
of the differences between apologetic and kerygmatic theology.[34]
He did not in general seem to draw a distinction between philo-

---

[32]S.T., I, p. 230.

[33]The Protestant Era, trans. James Luther Adams (abridged
ed.; Chicago: University of Chicago Press, 1957), pp. 83-84.

[34]S.T., I, pp. 4-8.

sophical and apologetic theology,[35] and thus we should hesitate
in considering philosophical theology to be only one kind of
apologetic theology, namely the kind which preaches to the intellectuals.

Indeed, we should not only hesitate but outrightly stop.
For Tillich quite plainly refuses to identify theology with
preaching or to judge a theology only by its "power" in attrac-
ting people to the Christian message. At the very outset of his
Systematic Theology, he states:

> Fundamentalists in America and orthodox theologians
> in Europe can point to the fact that their theology
> is eagerly received and held by many people just
> because of the historical or biographical situation
> in which men find themselves today. The fact is
> obvious but the interpretation is wrong. "Situa-
> tion" as one pole of theological work does not
> refer to the psychological or sociological state in
> which individuals or groups live. It refers to the
> scientific and artistic, the economic, political,
> and ethical forms in which they express their inter-
> pretations of existence. . . . Theology is neither
> preaching nor counselling; therefore the success of
> a theology when it is applied to preaching or the
> care of souls is not necessarily a criterion of its
> truth. The fact that fundamentalist ideas are
> eagerly grasped in a period of personal or communal
> disintegration does not prove their theological
> validity, just as the success of a liberal theology
> in periods of personal or communal integration is
> no certification of its truth. . . . The "situation"
> to which theology must respond is the totality of
> man's creative self-interpretation in a special
> period. Fundamentalism and orthodoxy reject this
> task, and in doing so, they miss the meaning of
> theology.[36] (italics mine)

These remarks entirely upset our cart, it would seem. Theology is not preaching. It is not to be judged by its power or
success, but by its truth or validity. Its aim is not merely
the pragmatic one of opening the Christian message to people,
but the apparently theoretical one of stating the message in correct form.

Indeed, this passage has such destructive implications for
our whole interpretation so far that we might do well to examine it more closely, in hopes of salvaging something. To begin
with, we can breathe a bit easier upon observing that Tillich
does not say that the success or apologetic power of a theology
is not at all a criterion of its truth, but that it is not necessarily a criterion of its truth. This qualification at least

---

[35]Cf. Theology of Culture, p. 127, where he speaks of "philosophical or apologetic theology."

[36]S.T., I, pp. 3-4.

blunts the edge of his attack. Furthermore, we can point to his
use of the term "truth" here; perhaps both apologetic power and
truth are the criteria of theology. On the basis of such obser-
vations alone, we might feel justified in not taking this passage as inconsistent with our previous conclusions.

Indeed, it simply cannot be denied that Tillich feels that
success, at least among the intellectuals, is part of the aim
and one of the criteria of theology. To deny this would be to
deny Tillich's own previous remarks. We must say, with respect
to fundamentalism, either that it is to be judged a failure
because it generally did not speak to the (or some) intellectuals,
or else that it was only a partial failure, satisfying the criterion of power but not of truth. (Indeed, these two possibilities may be identical.) The same remarks hold for liberalism,
insofar as it must be judged a failure.

We must say that Tillich's remarks here function not outrightly to negate the gist of our previous conclusions, but to
push us onward. The only point to be derived from them is that
there is some other criterion or criteria for theology than its
success--presumably even its success with the intellectuals.
But just what Tillich means by theological truth or validity is
not clear; to suggest as he does that theological validity is
judged by the adequacy of its response to "the totality of man's
creative self-interpretation" is to say little, if anything,
about any tolerably concrete, not to say meaningful, criteria.
It is also not clear how such a response to man's creative self-
interpretation would help serve the church.

In order to go further into Tillich's concept of the aim of
theology, it may be better to leave, for the time being, the
question of the value of ontology and ask a more fundamental question: the question of the value of dogma itself. We may then be
better equipped to deal with any further, non-apologetic functions
of ontology.

CHAPTER TWO

DOGMA: ITS TWO FUNCTIONS

A.   Dogma as Rational Thought about Faith

We have seen that Tillich gives, in part, an apologetic
answer to the question why it is necessary to think, or at least
to think ontologically, about faith. One reason theology uses
ontological concepts is that a certain segment of the population
uses them, and thus in order to best communicate with this group,
we must speak its language. But is there any further reason to
conceptualize? Are we, for example, somehow getting nearer to
the truth if we do, and if so, in what sense are we getting
nearer to the truth? And why is getting nearer to the truth
something valuable? What is good about truth?

By beginning with Tillich's remarks on ontological language,
we have gained some foothold on the question as to why theology
is necessary. But it is not a particularly firm foothold, for
we have only dealt with a few of Tillich's remarks about ontology. And furthermore, we are interested not only in the question why ontology is necessary in theology, but in the prior and
much broader question why any kind of rational thought about
faith is necessary. It may be helpful to ask Tillich simply how
any rational thought at all serves the church. We shall use as
our focal point some of Tillich's remarks about the value of
dogma.

One of Tillich's clearest statements on the nature and aim
of dogma occurs in his published lectures on The History of
Christian Thought, under the head "The Concept of Dogma." He
begins by saying that "all human experience implies the element
of thought," for man expresses himself in language and language
presupposes thought.[1] Hegel, in response to Schleiermacher's
view that feeling is essential to religion, said that dogs have
feeling but man has thought. Tillich states that this remark
of Hegel was based on a misunderstanding of what Schleiermacher
meant by "feeling" but he agrees with the main point: that
thought is essential to man and therefore to human religion.
Any man, "even the most pious Christian without any theological

---

[1]A History of Christian Thought, ed. Carl E. Braaten (New
York: Harper and Row, 1968), p. xi.

education," must think.[2] Universals or concepts are used "even at the most primitive levels of thought;"[3] as Clement of Alexandria said, the religion of animals would be wordless. Finally, Tillich observes that although reality precedes thought, thought also shapes reality, and this fact is significant for understanding the way in which doctrinal decisions have affected the lives of Christians.[4]

In all these remarks Tillich can be followed with some ease. If he wishes to remind his listeners, even those who profess a dislike for thought, that we can hardly be without it unless we return to the animal stage, we need not quibble. No doubt men generally use language and thus use thought, but what we are particularly interested in is the highly sophisticated, or at least rather odd, kind of thought which appears in theology. Tillich approaches the heart of the matter when he continues:

> There is also the development of methodological thought which proceeds according to the rules of logic and uses methods in order to deal with experiences. When this methodological thought is expressed in speaking or writing and communicated to other people, it produces theological doctrines. This is a development beyond the mere primitive use of thought. Ideally, such a development leads to a theological system.[5]

If we take these remarks together with the foregoing, we can say that Tillich has very roughly distinguished three levels of religious thought: the primitive (or ordinary), the dogmatic, and the systematic, each being somehow more logical or methodological than the preceding. We shall return later to the question of the nature and value of systematic thought; for now we are interested in dogmatic thought, which Tillich has described as thought about religion which "proceeds according to the rules of logic" and is "methodological." Perhaps we can say, in short, that dogma or doctrine is _rational_ thought about faith.

Thus the question, "Why do we need dogma?" becomes the question, "Why do we need rational thought?" Tillich goes on to say that dogma has two aims or functions: to express and to protect. It expresses what Christians accepted when they entered Christian congregations, somewhat similarly to the way in which

---

[2] Ibid., p. xi.

[3] Ibid., p. xi.

[4] Ibid., p. xi.

[5] Ibid., p. xii.

the dogmata of the ancient Greek schools such as the Peripatetics and Stoics expressed the fundamental presuppositions of the schools, so as to differentiate each from the others. And secondly, dogma functions to protect the substance of the biblical message against dangerous misinterpretations from those within the church.[6]

How much does this clarify our problem? Not much, I am afraid, although it may give us something to go on. Take first the idea that dogma expresses the Christian message. But, according to Tillich, the primitive level of thought had already expressed it. What is to be gained by expressing it more rationally? The fact that the ancient Greek schools also had dogmas which expressed their basic beliefs does not help, for why did they feel they had to have dogmas? Is it because they wanted to determine who did and who did not have the right to belong to their school? But why was this an important question? And how does dogma legitimately help answer it? Tillich has so far given no clear answer to the question why it is necessary for the Christian church to express rationally its fundamental beliefs. Why not express them irrationally or a-rationally, that is, say, in poetic or mythological or narrative forms?

Tillich elaborates upon this idea of dogma as expressive when he answers those among his listeners who feel hostile toward doctrinal examinations for the ministry. They should not forget, he says, that they "are entering a group which is different from other groups."[7] It is Christian, it is Catholic or Protestant, and "the church has a justified interest in having those who represent it show some acceptance of its foundations."[8] But again we must ask what this "justified interest" is. Tillich's next sentences apparently attempt to answer this, but they make matters worse instead of better: "Every baseball team demands that its members accept its rules and standards. Why should the church leave it completely to the arbitrary feelings of the individual? This is impossible."[9]

The comparison of the church to a baseball team is deflating. Is this as much of an answer as we can get from Tillich? Must we now try to figure out exactly why baseball teams need

---

[6]Ibid., pp. xiii-xiv.

[7]Ibid., p. xv.

[8]Ibid., pp. xv-xvi.

[9]Ibid., p. xvi.

rules, in what sense these rules are rational, and how these
rules are analogous to dogmas--and also why there <u>are</u> baseball
teams (and thus churches) in the first place? How seriously
should we take the analogy? The fact that it appears in a series
of lectures and is without obvious parallel in his books may be
reason for caution. At any rate, rather than indulging in speculation as to what Tillich was getting at, I suggest that we leave
the issue of dogma as expressive until we can find places where
Tillich clarifies himself. Instead, let us turn to his further
remarks here about the protective function of dogma.

Whereas the expressive function of dogma has to do with
differentiating the church from the world (as well as from other
churches), the protective function is a more internal matter.
Within the church itself, misinterpretations of the Christian
message arise, and dogma is needed to correct these misinterpretations. According to Tillich, "all dogmas were formulated negatively, that is, as reactions against misinterpretations from
inside the church."[10]   Dogmas are the result of life-and-death
struggles against those within the church who would misinterpret
the fundamental biblical message; for example, the first article
of the Apostle's Creed, affirming the belief that God is the
Creator of heaven and earth, is the rejection of a dualism which
threatened to undermine the substance of the Christian confession that Jesus was the Christ.[11]

> When new doctrines arose which seemed to undercut
> the fundamental confession, the protective doc-
> trines were added to it. In this way the dogmas
> arose. Luther recognized this fact that the dogmas
> were not the result of a theoretical interest,
> but arose from the need to protect the Christian
> substance.[12]

Tillich then explains why <u>philosophical</u> terms or concepts
were necessary in the dogmas:

> Since each new protective statement was itself
> subject to misinterpretation, there was always
> the need for sharper theoretical formulations.
> In order to do this it was necessary to use philo-
> sophical terms. This is how the many philosophical
> concepts entered into the Christian dogmas. Luther
> was very frank about this; he openly declared that
> he disliked terms like "trinity," "homoousion,"
> etc., but he admitted that they must be used[13] however
> unfortunate, because we have no better ones.

---

[10] <u>Ibid</u>., p. xiii.

[11] <u>Ibid</u>., p. xiv.

[12] Ibid., p. xiv.

[13] Ibid., p. xiv.

What Tillich is especially emphasizing in these remarks is most interesting. Dogma, in its protective role, seems to have the sole purpose of protecting against the prior formulation of bad doctrine. The suggestion is that rational and philosophical thought is necessary simply because of the presence within the church of people who, whether we like it or not, already use rational and philosophical thought, but use it in such a way as to endanger the Christian message. Reason, so to speak, must be fought with reason. Tillich concisely expresses this point in concluding his discussion of the protective or negative function of dogma: "Theoretical formulations must be made when other people formulate doctrines theoretically in such a way that the substance seems endangered."[14]

Of course, one cannot help wondering whether Tillich really agrees with Luther's dislike of philosophical terms, but this is not to the point. Whether or not Tillich is attracted to philosophical terminology, he here seems to claim that the church has no interest in this terminology as such, nor in rational thought in general. The church is interested in them because they must be used to avoid rational or philosophical distortions of the message. The individual theologian may have an interest in philosophy as such, but the church does not. The distinction between motives and reasons must be kept clear, if for no other reason than that Tillich himself apparently wishes to keep it clear.

But Tillich's remarks do raise at least one significant question. Dogmas function to protect, and what they protect against is misunderstanding of the Christian message. But precisely what is wrong with not understanding the Christian message? What is dangerous about it? For example, what is really dangerous about the dualism against which the doctrine of creation protects? A possible answer would be that such dualism is contrary to the fundamental Christian message, and if someone believes something contrary to the message he sins, endangering his immortal soul. But such a view of faith as believing certain things and of sin as not believing them smacks of the supranaturalism against which Tillich stands. What then is dangerous about misunderstanding the Christian message? Indeed, what is it to misunderstand the message, since even the theologians, who are supposed to help us to understand it properly, disagree profoundly among themselves as to what the message is.

---

[14]Ibid., p. xiv.

Such questions indicate that we must not rest any more satisfied with Tillich's discussion of the protective function of
dogma than with his discussion of its expressive function. Let
us see what further light can be shed on Tillich's concept of
dogma by examining other parts of his works.

B. Dogma: Its Expressive Function

Tillich has suggested that one of the functions of dogma is
to express, in rational concepts, the Christian message. But
why should the church wish to express itself in this way? Perhaps we might be satisfied with his claim that the church has to
distinguish itself in some way from other groups, though the problem of exclusivism which arises here is irritable. But the
question which is particularly relevant to us is why rational and
eventually philosophical concepts and ways of thinking must be
used. Although the Judaism of the Old Testament had certain
means to determine who was and who was not a Jew, it apparently
made little use of abstract and ontological reflection for this,
or any other, purpose.

Indeed, I am not at all sure that Tillich does justice to
himself when he suggests that the expressive function of dogma
not only once was but still is best founded upon the need to
determine who has the right to be a member of the church. For
Tillich was singularly uninterested in anything which approached
an authoritarian or exclusivist solution to such a problem. His
own criterion for determining who has the right to belong to the
church is as loose and anti-exclusive as it could be: the individual needs only decide "whether he wishes to belong or not to
belong to a community which asserts that Jesus is the Christ."[15]
One need not even accept this assertion oneself![16] Tillich
apparently would allow anybody to be a member of the church who
wishes to be a member. When then should the church today feel
it has to think rationally about its message? Do Tillich's two
reasons for dogma finally reduce to one? Can we say that the
only reason for dogma is to protect? Of course, to state a dogma at all, even with the purpose of protecting, necessarily
involves expressing it; that is a trivial point. It is obvious
that to have dogma at all means one has to express it. The
question is whether this expression has any other aim than to
protect.

---

[15]S.T., III, pp. 174-175.

[16]Ibid., p. 174.

I believe it has, for Tillich, and I believe he was trying
to say so when he made the distinction in the lectures we have
examined. He makes himself much clearer on the point when discussing, in the Systematic Theology, the Christological dogma.
Here again he states that we must ask two questions about dogma:
"To what degree did dogma succeed in reaffirming the genuine
meaning of the Christian message against actual and threatening
distortions? And how successful was the conceptualization of
the symbols expressing the Christian message?"[17] He repeats this
distinction several times, even putting it in terms of his fundamental distinction between substance and form:

> In discussing the christological dogma the
> following questions must be asked: Does the
> dogmatic statement accomplish what it is sup-
> posed to, namely to reaffirm the message of
> Jesus as the Christ against actual distortions
> and to provide a conceptually clear expression
> of the meaning of the message? In this respect,
> a dogmatic statement can fail in two possible
> ways. It can fail in both its substance and
> its conceptual form.[18]

And again, Tillich asserts that there are two kinds of attack on
the basic Christian affirmation that Jesus is the Christ: "Some
of them are on its substance, e.g. the baptismal confession, and
some of them are on its form, as in the use of Greek concepts."[19]

I believe that the two criteria Tillich is speaking of here
are simply re-statements of the expressive and protective criteria. The one criterion has to do with protecting the message
against distortion; the other with giving an adequate conceptual
expression of the message. And the criteria, furthermore, are
quite distinct, for Tillich states that while Chalcedon's doctrine of the two natures of Christ succeeded in protecting (i.e.
in its substance), it did not succeed in adequately expressing
(i.e. in its conceptual form). It did not give an adequate conceptual expression of the Christian message.

How then did Chalcedon fail? What is it, and why is it
important, to give an adequate conceptualization of the Christian message? Tillich here says nothing about baseball teams or
the question of church membership; rather, his answer, so far as
I can see, is the following: "In order to be received, the
church had to use the forms of life and thought which were crea-

---

[17] S.T., II, p. 140.

[18] Ibid., p. 141.

[19] Ibid., p. 139.

ted by the various sources of Hellenism and which coalesced at
the end of the ancient world"[20] (italics mine). The use of Greek
concepts taken from the philosophical schools of antiquity was
"inescapable in the church's missionary activity in the Hellenistic world"[21] (italics mine).

This is a rather surprising answer. For it returns us precisely to where we began: one conceptualizes and uses reason and
philosophy for apologetic purposes; that is, "in order to be
received." As carefully as we listen to Tillich here, we do not
find the answer that we would perhaps expect: that philosophical
language can somehow be a more literal or intrinsically more true
or adequate or valid expression of the Christian faith. Rational
and philosophical language is used because it is the language of
one's listeners (presumably the intellectuals: Tillich hardly
has to point out that the ordinary Greek would have little understood the abstractions of Chalcedon). Rational and philosophical
concepts are the concepts they understand. Insofar as the church
must speak to the intellectuals, such language is necessary simply
in order to communicate.

Of course, to say that philosophical or conceptual language
is more rational than religious or symbolic language may be true,
but only because it is an empty tautology. To say more than this,
though, for example that it expresses the Christian faith in a
truly more adequate way, is to say too much. It is indeed true
that through conceptualization the message is expressed in an
intellectually or rationally more adequate way; but that is only
to say that through conceptualization the message is expressed
more adequately to the intellectuals. But this is remarkably
like saying that we can express the Christian faith to a Navajo
in his own language better than we can express it to him in English. It is strictly a matter of communication, of apologetics,
not of truth.

Why then did Chalcedon fail? For it surely made use of
conceptual language. Tillich's apparent answer is that it vio-
lated the very rules that its chosen apologetic language
required of it: it fell into contradictions, the one thing that
Greek philosophical language rules out more than anything else.
Chalcedon was inadequate because it stated (and protected) the
message only "through an accumulation of powerful paradoxa. It
was unable to give a constructive interpretation, although this
was just the reason for the original introduction of the philo-

---

[20]Ibid., p. 141.

[21]Ibid., pp. 140-141.

sophical concepts."[22] The two-nature theory was driven into
"inescapable contradictions and absurdities."[23]

And do we detect in the words "constructive interpretation"
a suggestion to see in rational and ontological thinking some
"higher" function than the apologetic one? Is there the suggestion that giving a constructive interpretation is another reason
for using philosophical concepts? No, for Tillich states that
this reason is identical with the reason for "the original introduction of the philosophical concepts," and as we have already
seen, this reason was simply an apologetic one, "inescapable in
the church's missionary activity in the Hellenistic world." We
might say that the theoretical receives its justification from
the fact that, for some, it is existential.[24]

Thus we seem to have made little progress. Tillich's "expressive" function of dogma or rational thought about faith is
really our old one, the apologetic function. Let us turn, then,
to the other function of dogma, the protective.

C. Dogma: Its Protective Function

1. Protection, absurdity, and apologetics. Perhaps if we
examine Tillich's protective criterion for the proper use of dogma, we will discover something new. One of the reasons the
church has for using dogma or rational thought is to protect
against distorted doctrines which may arise in the church itself.
But just what makes a doctrine distorted? A distorted doctrine,
Tillich has told us, scmehow leads to misunderstanding. In
order for a Christian to properly understand his faith, proper
doctrine is necessary. But what is it to understand the Christian faith? Why must one understand it properly? Would it not
be possible to be a good Christian even if one expressed his
faith quite unphilosophically and irrationally, breaking all the
rules of logic? Why should we fear this? For Christianity is

---

[22]Ibid., pp. 141-142. It is noteworthy that Tillich does
not think that Chalcedon could have avoided the paradoxes: "It
could not have done otherwise within the conceptual frame used"
(p. 141). This inherent inadequacy of Greek concepts to express
the Christian message is somehow related to their derivation
from "a concrete religion determined by the divine figures of
Apollo and Dionysus" (p. 140). One wishes Tillich had said more
about this.

[23]Ibid., p. 146.

[24]Cf. S.T., III, p. 5, where Tillich says that philosophical questions are often asked "with existential urgency and out
of cognitive honesty. And the lack of an adequate answer can
become a stumbling block for a man's whole religious life."

not a matter of "information" but of being grasped by our ultimate concern, the New Being in Jesus as the Christ.

Tillich sometimes suggests that one kind of distortion that
conceptualization protects us against is literalism. "We have
discussed the symbols--Son of Man, Son of God, the Christ, the
Logos--in four steps, of which the last was the literalistic distortion. This danger--which is always present in Christianity--
was one of the reasons why the early church began to interpret
the Christological symbols in conceptual terms available through
the work of Greek philosophy."[25] Here is an important clue.
Now if we can discover what is wrong with literalism, we may be
able to see in what way rational and ontological concepts protect us from it.

Tillich has a great deal to say about literalism and its
theological ally, supranaturalism, and his most frequent charge
against their tenets is that they are blatantly irrational, ridiculous, superstitious, and, most commonly, absurd. The Christological symbols, he says, fall into "absurdity and superstition"
if interpreted literally.[26] He observes that the idea of Christ
sitting at the right hand of God is, if taken literally, "absurd
and ridiculous."[27] Concerning the story of the Ascension, he
says: "If taken literally, its spatial symbolism would become
absurd."[28] Literalism makes the symbol "Son of Man" into the
basis for "an absurd story,"[29] and literalistic interpretations
of the term "Son of God" must be rejected as "superstitious."[30]
The idea that only a small number of people will ever reach salvation is "absurd and demonic."[31] The attempt of some orthodox
theologians to consider Adam as perfect is "absurd."[32] The view
of Biblical literalism that the Fall of man changed the structures of nature is to be "rejected as absurd."[33] God's omnipo-

---

[25] S.T., II, p. 139.

[26] Ibid., p. 113; cf. also pp. 155-156.

[27] Ibid., p. 162.

[28] Ibid., p. 162.

[29] Ibid., p. 109.

[30] Ibid., p. 110.

[31] Ibid., p. 167.

[32] Ibid., p. 34.

[33] Ibid., p. 40.

tence is not to be interpreted literally as the ability of a highest being to do anything he wishes, for this would be "magic and an absurdity";[34] it leads into "a fog of absurd imaginations."[35] Various literalistic doctrines which try to deny both the threat of hell and the certainty of salvation, such as the ideas of reincarnation, of an intermediary state, and of purgatory, fall into "a complete absurdity" in the case of "infants, children, and undeveloped adults."[36]

Thus we can state unequivocally that Tillich thinks that literalism is absurd. He gives a resoundingly clear answer to our question, "What is wrong with literalism?" Its sin is absurdity. But our questioning cannot stop here, for we must next ask what is wrong with absurdity in theology. This may itself seem an absurd question; in everyday life if an individual concocts the absurd idea that he can fly off tall buildings, he is in serious danger. But religious beliefs or doctrines are not of this nature, according to Tillich; they are not matters of information or fact. Furthermore, Tillich is surely aware that certain theologians, such as Tertullian, Luther, Kierkegaard, and Barth, had such contempt for rationality and philosophy as to delight in observing the absurdity, the paradoxical nature, or the "impossibility" of what the Christian faith affirms. That is, they simply reject Tillich's presupposition that absurdity is illegitimate in theology and with it any arguments involving the charge of absurdity. The argument that it is absurd to believe literally in the Incarnation or the Resurrection would carry no weight with them. Indeed, some of these theologians come near to speaking as if the demonstration that a belief is, by rational (i.e. human) standards, absurd would be evidence in favor of the belief. If Tillich and his opponents simply have different criteria, why then should Tillich argue with them? Indeed, how can he argue with them? How can he hope to convince them?

To answer such questions, we must ask why Tillich is against absurdity. In what danger is the church if it states, and takes literally, its belief in, say, the Resurrection or any number of other miracles? What is really wrong if an individual Christian thinks of God quite literally sitting above the clouds in heaven,

---

[34]S.T., I, pp. 273-274; cf. also Brown, pp. 169-170.

[35]Love, Power, and Justice: Ontological Analyses and Ethical Implications (New York: Oxford University Press, 1954), p. 110.

[36]S.T., III, p. 416.

with Christ at his right hand? Granted that these beliefs, or some of them, may have to be classed as absurd, but so what? Who is getting hurt by them? And indeed, are any other beliefs or doctrines more _true_? Are not even the most abstract philosophical statements about God also symbolic and thus not to be taken literally?

Sometimes Tillich claims that literalism has less _power_ than the symbolic understanding of religious language. It objectifies the Christian message and thus is not "existential" or "existentially meaningful." Classical theologians, he says, were aware that the aim of the symbolic interpretation of religious assertions is "to give to God and to all his relations to man more reality and power than a nonsymbolic and therefore easily superstitious interpretation could give them."[37] Such an interpretation "enhances rather than diminishes the reality and power of religious language, and in so doing it performs an important function."[38] We should never say "only a symbol," because that indicates a misunderstanding of the fact that symbolic language "surpasses in quality and strength the power of any non-symbolic language."[39] Concerning the religious symbols related to the Resurrection, Tillich says, "Their power must be reestablished by a reinterpretation which unites cosmic and existential qualities."[40] Tillich calls supranaturalism (which he virtually identifies with literalism) "a rationalization of the Biblical symbols into an objectifying description of physical-supraphysical processes,"[41] and such rationalization and objectification stand in direct contrast to the "existential-symbolic" character of religious assertions.[42]

What are we to make of all this? Somehow, through all this talk of power and existential significance, Tillich seems to be speaking of the problem more commonly known as the problem of "relevance." But is that not an _apologetic_ problem? Can Tillich be suggesting that literalism is bad because it leads to absurd-

---

[37]_S.T._, I, p. 241.

[38]_Ibid._, p. 241.

[39]_Dynamics of Faith_, p. 45.

[40]_S.T._, II, p. 164.

[41]Charles W. Kegley and Robert W. Bretall (eds.), _The Theology of Paul Tillich_ (New York: The Macmillan Co., 1956), p. 341.

[42]_S.T._, II, p. 127.

ity, and absurdity is bad because it leads to rejection of the Christian message?

Tillich's own words strongly support such a view. "The symbols have been greatly distorted and consequently were rejected by many because of a literalism which makes them absurd and nonexistential"[43] (italics mine). Literalism, he says in one of his essays, leads to absurdities, and this "is one of the reasons for the destruction of religion through wrong communicative interpretation of it."[44] We must avoid literalism, else "our contemporaries will rightly turn away from us as from people who still live in absurdities and superstitions."[45] Again, literalism makes the Christological symbols "an unnecessary stumbling block."[46] And Tillich makes quite clear the apologetic danger of literalism when he states: "Theology need not take literalism seriously, but we must realize how its impact has hanpered the apologetic task of the Christian church."[47]

Thus literalism, because of its absurdity, lacks power, and what lacks power turns people away; or, to speak more precisely, what turns people away is what, by definition, lacks power. For something to lack power or to be non-existential is for it to be rejected or ignored as something one does not care about or with which one is not concerned. And the Christian message is not being served if it is so stated as to make God, the object of our ultimate concern, into something of little concern.

But can Tillich seriously maintain that literalism and supranaturalism--or any other forms of absurdity, for that matter--lack power? For if they do, what is he so upset about? Why does he spend so much of his time combatting them if their absurdity is so patent that they can exert no significant power? Can it be denied that literalism, in the form, say, of American fundamentalism, is extremely powerful, existential, and "relevant" to some people? Surely Tillich is aware of the high passion of a revival meeting. Indeed, we have seen that he plainly admits that fundamentalism sometimes has tremendous power.[48]

But these questions are easily resolved if we remember to

---

[43] S.T., II, p. 164.

[44] Theology of Culture, p. 62.

[45] Ibid., p. 63.

[46] S.T., II, p. 112.

[47] Ibid., p. 29.

[48] S.T., I, p. 4; see above, p. 12.

whom Tillich insists he is mainly addressing himself: the intellectuals. It is to them that literalism lacks power, and it
lacks power precisely because of its absurdity or irrationality.
Countless other people may not consider literalism absurd and
thus it may have great power for them, but the intellectuals are,
virtually by definition, precisely that group which is especially
offended by absurdity. A child can be moved by the idea of
Santa Claus, even though he does not understand in the least; a
literalist may be moved by the idea of God doing miracles and
turning into a man, even though it is unexplainable, a mystery;
but the intellectual cannot be moved by what he cannot understand
or make rational sense of--and Christianity is supposed to speak
to all men, even "the people who cannot escape the sad destiny
of having to think."[49] The purpose of avoiding literalism, in
other words, again is not a theoretical but a practical purpose,
and more specifically an apologetic one. We have still not seen
Tillich state that a theological (or conceptual, or non-absurd)
formulation of the Christian message is in any respect inherently
better than a literalist, or for that matter a Navajo, formulation, nor that the intellectual's way of thinking is any more
valid than the child's. It is simply different. And theology,
the logos of theos, the rational word about God, is the expression of the word to rational men.

    This can hardly be the end of the matter, but before pro-
ceeding, it may be worthwhile to clarify what may seem an oddity
in Tillich's concept of dogma as we have thus far examined it.
Tillich has claimed that dogma is the attempt to think rationally
about the Christian message, and yet dogma is very often looked
upon (and even defined) as a body of strange, unintelligible
assertions with little obvious relation to rational thought at
all. But this can be easily explained by Tillich as due to
nothing but a change in the situation, which means, in this context, a change in the way of thinking of the intellectuals.
Each generation has its own particular ways of thought, its own
conceptual framework. In the early and medieval church, Greek
and Latin concepts were most intelligible to the educated men,
and thus the church used them in its missionary work with the
intellectuals. What has happened, however, is that these old
ways of thought have become static in the church, while the outside world has changed its ways of thought. Thus the original
purpose for which particular dogmas were introduced into the

---

[49]Brown, p. 190.

church is no longer served if the intellectual climate changes, and this obviously means that the old dogmas have to be re-interpreted, i.e., reformulated, in terms intelligible to the intellectuals of today. The old formulations no longer serve their apologetic purpose; thus the need for new thought.[50]

2. Truth and consequences. Surely, however, we have still not done full justice to Tillich's concept of the protective role of dogma. We have, indeed, succeeded only in reducing the two roles of dogma to one: the apologetic. On the basis of Tillich's own words, we have been able so to interpret the concept of "protecting" as to mean "protecting against rejection by the intellectuals." This has had the advantage of allowing us to see the extensiveness of Tillich's use of the apologetic criterion, but it simply does not do justice to Tillich's intent. For Tillich's main point about the protective function of dogma was that it somehow serves to protect the church itself, and not just against rejection by a certain group. One might say that Tillich apparently thinks that the church itself has something to learn from culture, and especially from its own rejection by culture. It is not just a bare apologetic fact that the intellectuals reject absurdity and irrationality; it is a significant fact. Irrationality endangers the church itself.

But we must not think that absurdity is the only theological danger, any more than literalism is. Tillich has stated that dogma in its protective function has to do with preserving the substance of the Christian message against distortion, and surely human ingenuity has not confined itself merely to absurdity in producing distortions of the message. For example, Tillich was strongly opposed to the liberalism of the Ritschlian school, and yet he does not accuse it of absurdity. The same could be said of many other views he rejects.

Perhaps we could begin a more serious analysis of Tillich's view of the protective function of dogma by asking precisely what it is that dogma protects against. Of course, it would be easy to take Tillich's statements that dogma protects against distortions and misunderstandings of the Christian message as the answer we seek. But is it altogether clear just what is involved in distorting or misunderstanding the Christian message? What is it to misunderstand the message? Is it to believe something false? And if so, how does one decide what is false? And once one decides, how does one show that such falsehood is somehow dangerous to the church?

---

[50] Ibid., pp. 65-66.

It is true that Tillich sometimes speaks as if misunderstanding or distorting the Christian message is simply a matter of believing what is false. He sometimes suggests that dogma, whether directed against supranaturalism or any number of other errors, protects from false beliefs. For example, Tillich states that theological theism, in maintaining that God is a being and not being-itself, must be rejected not because it is irrelevant, and not because it is one-sided, but "because it is wrong. It is bad theology."[51] The same holds for the belief in "objective" miracles; Tillich seems to think that it is simply false that the laws of nature can be disrupted.[52] Similarly, the dogma of creation ex nihilo is "not a description of the way God creates, but a protective concept that is only negatively meaningful."[53] This dogma protects against all types of ultimate dualism, as found in ancient paganism and Gnosticism, which affirm " a prior resisting matter out of which God created the world" and thus endanger the fundamental Christian affirmation that creation is good.[54]

Thus the Christian apparently must not believe in God as a highest being, in objective miracles, or in dualism. But one wonders why not? What makes Tillich so sure that God is not a highest being, and by what special insight does he determine that objective miracles simply cannot occur? And furthermore, what is dangerous about such false beliefs? Is a Platonist, who believes in a prior resisting matter shaped by the Demiurge, in mortal danger simply because he believes the wrong thing?

Of course, one possible answer to such questions would be that such beliefs are contrary to the true Christian message. Although they cannot be proved false, they can be shown to be inconsistent with the message, so that if the message is accepted, views such as dualism must be rejected, and since one's salvation depends upon accepting the Christian message, heretical views must be rejected as dangerous. But I rather doubt that such a way of thinking is at the root of Tillich's theology, and even if it were, the questions that arise are so numerous that our attempt to make some sense of Tillich would seem futile. For how does one determine what Christianity, or the true or funda-

---

[51]The Courage to Be (New Haven: Yale University Press, 1952), p. 184.

[52]S.T., I, p. 115.

[53]A History of Christian Thought, p. 42; cf. also S.T., I, p. 253.

[54]Ibid., p. 42; cf. also pp. 20-21; S.T., I, p. 253.

mental Christian message, really is? Nobody can fail to observe
that theologians disagree about this, but the further question
could be asked: how can they possibly ever overcome their disagreements? What possible arguments could help settle the matter?
Where shall we look to find what God is trying to tell us? If
we look to the Bible alone, we may already have lost the Roman
Catholics and those who wish to look at tradition too, but even
so, what part of the Bible shall we especially attend to? If
we say that Paul is somehow most significant, we can ask what
part of Paul. And once we have settled such questions, whose
interpretation of Paul shall we use? Our own interpretation?
But that seems strangely subjective, and at any rate such an
approach would have little potential for settling the issue with
those who differ. Luther's interpretation, then? But why
Luther? And whose interpretation of Luther shall we use?

Such questions are not meant to be flippant. No doubt they
can be answered; indeed, they can be answered in countless ways,
embarrassing us with riches. What is puzzling about them is
that it is hard to make out what is at stake. What if someone
suggests, for example, that Calvin's theology, or a part of it,
is not truly Christian, and that against him we must produce or
reproduce doctrine that is truly Christian, in order to save the
Christian message from being distorted or falsely proclaimed.
The mob of questions that arise about the nature of true Christianity and the means of discovering it push us to the prior
question: what is being asked (or, alternatively, what is being
answered)? If one fights Calvin by quoting Augustine, or John
by quoting Paul, have we then determined what the Christian message is? Or have we not merely pre-determined what it is? If
someone says that Calvin's theology was not Christian, is he
really saying that Calvin's theology is contrary to Augustine's
theology? When Tillich says that supranaturalism is a distortion of the Christian message, is he saying that it is a distortion of Luther or Paul (or, worse, of his own interpretation of
Luther or Paul)? But how is he so sure that Luther was right,
or Paul for that matter?

It should be noted that the issue here is not merely why
theologians disagree, or whether in fact they do, to some extent,
predetermine or "pre-understand" their views. Perhaps there is
even something good about disagreement. Rather, the issue has
to do with why theologians act as if their disagreements could
be rationally overcome; i.e., why they argue. So long as theology is givena strictly apologetic function, the differences

32

between theologians can be seen as different expressions or formulations of the Christian message; that is, the differences are
not of great significance, as Tillich himself suggested in his
remarks on Barth and other theologians.[55]   Indeed, even arguments among theologians could be explained as, so to speak, rhetorical arguments: it may unfortunately be necessary to offer
"arguments" against other theologians simply because one's listeners may listen more carefully if one first takes pains to
disassociate oneself from those whose way of thinking they des-
pise. But such "arguments" would be no more serious than those,
say, between different politicians who, though they may agree,
find that their different constituencies necessitate at least
seeming to disagree--and all this for the ultimate good, getting
the bill passed or the message understood.

Thus if theologians truly agree, it is difficult to take
seriously their arguments and debates, and if they truly disagree,
it is difficult to see how their arguments could succeed in
bringing agreement. What then could Tillich's so-called protective criterion for dogma be? How could it function as a serious
criterion or as the basis for a serious argument?

Perhaps we can begin to get some hold on Tillich's views
here by again confining ourselves to one of the views he rejects,
literalism, and to one of his reasons for rejecting it, its
absurdity. For not only does he apparently think that absurdity
is especially dangerous, but I daresay the ordinary run of theologians today, however much they might differ as to whether, say,
Luther or Calvin is more decisive for the proper understanding
of Christianity, at least agree that manifest absurdity of the
type represented by those who take literally, say, the Creation
story, is to be rejected. What we wish to discover are the
non-apologetic reasons why literalism and absurdity in general
might be dangerous, or why, so to speak, the literalist himself
is in danger.

We have already seen that one of Tillich's main arguments
against literalism is that it is absurd. But in order to determine why absurdity is dangerous, we must first try to determine
more carefully just what absurdity, for Tillich, is. For we
have thus far looked at absurdity from the outside, so to speak;
we have not found what absurdity is but only that it is one of
the things that offend the intellectuals. But what are they
offended about?

---

[55]See above, pp. 5-6.

Since Tillich so often uses the notion of absurdity in
rejecting literalism, we might expect him to somewhere define
what he means by the term. But although he explicitly deals
with the concept at one point in the Systematic Theology, his
discussion is not particularly helpful. In discussing the various distortions of the Christian concept of paradox, he notes
that the absurd is often confused with it, partly due to the
phrase wrongly attributed to Tertullian, credo quia absurdum.
He then offers an apparent definition of absurdity:

> Combinations of logically compatible words become
> absurd when they contradict the meaningful order
> of reality. Therefore, the absurd lies in the
> neighborhood of the grotesque and the ridiculous.
> We have used this term several times in rejecting
> symbolic literalism and its grotesque consequences.
> Such absurdities, however, have no relation to the
> paradox of the Christian message.[56]

It is most interesting that Tillich uses the terms "gro-
tesque" and "ridiculous" to describe absurdity, since they help
support our above apologetic view of absurdity: absurdity is
offensive to some men. But his basic definition of absurdity is
given in the first sentence. An absurd assertion is not self-
contradictory (nor is it mere semantic nonsense[57]); it is a consistent assertion which contradicts the meaningful order of
reality. This is not, however, a particularly clear definition.
What is "the meaningful order of reality?" Furthermore, Tillich's
definition of absurdity seems to conflict with his definition of
irrationality on the same page; he says that the irrational is
to be accepted as an unexplainable fact; it expresses man's
fallenness, the transition from essence to existence: "It is an
undeniable fact which must be accepted, although it contradicts
the essential structure of everything created."[58] Thus we must
accept the irrational and reject the absurd, even though both
have to do with contradicting the meaningful order (or essential
structure) of reality. The absurd cannot happen: the irrational
not only can happen but has happened, in the form of sin or
estrangement.

Are we to see theology reduced to rhetoric here? Are we to
say that man's fallenness is acceptable today, since many intel-

---

[56] S.T., II, p. 91.

[57] Ibid., p. 91. Tillich deals separately with "nonsense"
as a distortion of the paradox, thus indicating that absurdity
and nonsense are not the same thing.

[58] Ibid., p. 91.

34

lectuals accept it, while miracles are to be rejected, since
most intellectuals reject them--even though both radical evil and
objective miracles are equally irrational and (or) absurd?

Perhaps if we remember some of Tillich's examples of
absurdity, we can better understand him. One of the most common
kinds of thing Tillich classes as absurd is the belief in various
views which conflict with the scientific view of reality. For
example, some of the instances already given of beliefs Tillich
considers to be absurd seem to derive their absurdity from taking
spatial symbols literally (e.g., the idea that Jesus was the Son
of God who, in the Incarnation, came from and, in the Ascension,
returned to a place in the sky called Heaven). Why is it absurd
to take such ideas literally? In speaking of God's relation to
space and of the spatial symbols found in Christianity, Tillich
gives us an answer:

> In a vision of the universe which has no basis for
> a tripartite view of cosmic space in terms of earth,
> heaven, and underworld, theology must emphasize the
> symbolic character of spatial symbols, in spite of
> their rather literal use in Bible and cult. Almost
> every Christian doctrine has been shaped by these
> symbols and needs reformulation in the light of a
> spatially monistic universe. "God is in heaven";
> this means that his life is qualitatively different
> from creaturely existence. But it does not mean
> that he "lives in" or "descends from" a special
> place.[59]

Here Tillich claims that spatial symbolism, which, as we
have seen, is absurd if taken literally, is to be rejected
because it conflicts with the scientific world view. Perhaps we
can take this to mean that absurdity is, at least in part, what
conflicts with science. Such an interpretation is corroborated
by Tillich's remarks about the absurdity of the physical theory
of the Resurrection. If such a theory is accepted, "the absurd
question arises as to what happened to the molecules which com-
prise the corpse of Jesus."[60] We might wonder why Tillich calls
the question absurd, since it seems to be quite a reasonable one,
but Tillich plainly means that the belief itself is absurd--and
it is absurd because it is scientifically objectionable.

Indeed, not only Tillich's criticism of the Resurrection
but his view of miracles in general seems based on the scientific attitude. His lengthy debate with students and professors
recorded in Ultimate Concern clearly shows this. He says that
if miracle stories are told, "we have to inquire historically as

---

[59] S.T., I, p. 277.

[60] S.T., II, p. 156.

to the real basis for them."[61] When asked whether the "levita-
tion" stories in various religious traditions might not be true,
he answers as the good, tough-minded scientist: "I would insist
first on some historical research. How well authenticated are
the documents?"[62] And while noting that certain so-called scientific explanations of miracles "are sometimes more fantastic than
the stories themselves,"[63] he suggests that the parting of the
Red Sea may have been due to tides and storms,[64] and he outrightly
claims that "what actually happened seems clear" in the story of
God's salvation of Jerusalem in the time of Isaiah: "An epidemic
attack of cholera, or something like it, killed many of the sol-
diers and officers, and so the king of Assyria decided that with
his limited power he could not take Jerusalem."[65]

Thus Tillich takes science and its method very seriously,
and absurdity seems to be a matter of not doing so. But one wonders how taking science seriously serves the church. The apologetic answer is obvious: if Tillich is speaking to scientists
and those who accept science, his arguments showing the absurdity
of literalism, while in a logical sense being unnecessary (since
his listeners already think literalism absurd and therefore
offensive), might be rhetorically (or psychologically) necessary
to assure his listeners that he agrees, and agrees for the same
reasons, with their rejection of literalism.

But what protective answer does Tillich give to the question of the value of the scientific view of the miraculous?
Indeed, we might ask what possible answer Tillich could give.
For he would presumably be speaking to the literalists, or to
those tempted by it, and how could any arguments here succeed?
Does not Tillich simply presuppose the validity of natural science, while the literalist rejects this presupposition? How
would Tillich answer a literalist critic who said that, when
forced to choose between Scripture and science, one should choose
Scripture? If Tillich answered that this would be absurd, he
would be arguing in a circle, for absurdity seems simply to mean
that which conflicts with science, and his critic is well aware
of this conflict.

---

[61]Brown, p. 161.

[62]Ibid., p. 165.

[63]Ibid., p. 168.

[64]Ibid.

[65]Ibid.

Does reason (in the sense of "reasoning together") break down here? Does the matter come to this: that Tillich chooses one side, his opponents the other, and that is the end of the matter? Would any arguments be relevant to the solution of such a conflict?

Of course, Tillich could say that he believes in the scientific method because it is based on solid evidence and self-criticism,[66] but this need not deter the literalist; he could merely point out that Tillich is again repeating himself, i.e., arguing in a circle. For the basic question is whether things like evidence and self-criticism are to be taken as ultimately authoritative. The whole question is whether or not to accept science and its method, and if the matter boils down to a difference of presuppositions, how is argument possible? Why does Tillich make it sound as if he is <u>refuting</u> the literalist, rather than just <u>differing</u> with him? His arguments would fall dead at the feet of any literalist who is aware that he is not being rational in the scientific sense. If this is the kind of thing that goes on in theological debate, no wonder it is fruitless, for the disputants have different starting points; they lack a common ground. But then another wonder appears: why do theologians not realize this and cease their arguing about such matters, since no argument could hope to succeed?

We are thus faced with two questions: what danger is the literalist in, and how could any argument with him hope to succeed? Our immediate task is to answer the first question, but our ultimate aim is to answer the second--and we might expect, or at least hope, that the two answers are related.

How shall we get some solid foothold here? We have observed that if Tillich is speaking to the alienated intellectuals, his arguments against literalism on the grounds of its absurdity would be unnecessary <u>as</u> <u>arguments</u>, since these people already accept such arguments. By the same token, if he is speaking to the thoroughgoing literalist, his arguments would be futile, since the literalist has different presuppositions. But is there not a third group to whom Tillich might be speaking, namely, those who stand "on the boundary" between the literalistic and the scientific approach? I refer here not so much to those who cannot decide which way to leap, but to those who have already found a resting place in the conviction that their literalistic beliefs are <u>compatible</u> <u>with</u> science. Here we could distinguish various

---

[66]<u>S.T.</u>, II, p. 103.

levels of sophistication. No doubt one first calls to mind the
various attempts to find Noah's ark or to give historical or
even physical evidence for various miracles reported in Scripture
and tradition. Such attempts have not been notable for their
success, especially among respectable theologians. But there
are many distinguished theologians whose aim is not to provide
scientific evidence for miraculous or otherwise strange stories,
but to show that there is no inconsistency between the acceptance of science and the belief in these events. Here one enters
the very complex issues of what science does and does not allow
for, and perhaps eventually the discussion would be led to semantic investigations regarding the meaning of words such as "science," "evidence," and "rationality," on the one hand, and "miracle," "act of God," and "faith" on the other.

I suspect that here we approach more closely to Tillich's
line of thought. But we must note that the fact remains that
he does not consider many of the complexities of these issues.
He adamantly refuses to accept the view that objective miracles
can happen; he does not furnish a serious analysis of the concept of science upon which his certainty seems based. He simply
refuses to take the literalistic belief in miracles seriously.[67]
Tillich seems to be quite the orthodox scientist here; indeed,
we might even call him a dogmatic scientist. He rejects the
belief in objective miracles without, apparently, seriously considering the evidence for or even the possibility of particular
miracles. He seems to be in principle or a priori against such
events.

At this point we could ask whether such dogmatic scientism
is itself scientific. How can anyone be so sure that objective
miracles do not happen? Has Tillich simply closed his mind to
such possibilities, and if so, is this the mark of rationality?
Would it not be more rational and more scientific to reject only
specific miracles (on the basis of insufficient evidence) but
never to reject miracles in general?

The question that arises here is whether Tillich in fact
rejects objective miracles in principle, but the prior question
is what he means by an "objective miracle." He seems to mean
by this term a suspension of the laws of nature.[68] But is he
speaking here of the known laws of nature or of all possible

---

[67]Ibid., p. 29: "Theology need not take literalism seriously."

[68]S.T., I, pp. 115, 117; Brown, pp. 158-159.

laws of nature? Is he, for example, saying that faith healing
or water walking are impossible, or is he saying that such things
have not been adequately evidenced, and that if they were authenticated they still would have to follow some natural laws?

Tillich is not saying the former, and I doubt that any scientist would. The whole history of science has been a confron-
tation with events which contradict the known laws of nature,
and science has progressed by finding new laws or explanations.
What Tillich and the scientists seem to be objecting to is the
view that things can happen which are in principle unexplainable
by science. Tillich is apparently against the belief that things
can happen which cannot possibly be explained. He is not rejecting the possibility of any specific events. He makes this quite
clear in speaking of the proper attitude of historical science
toward miracles:

> The historical method approaches the miracle
> stories neither with the assumption that they
> happened because they are attributed to him who
> is called the Christ nor with the assumption
> that they have not happened because such events
> contradict the laws of nature.[69]

Thus the scientist remains open to the possibility of certain events. Perhaps here is the crux of the issue between
Tillich and the literalist. For the literalist wishes to hold
that certain events have occurred which contradict all possible
laws of nature. He would not be satisfied if it were shown that
a specific event reported in the Bible, such as an instance of
faith healing, did occur but can be explained by contemporary
psychology. He would not be satisfied with Tillich's admission
that the Red Sea may indeed have parted, but due to natural
causes. He wishes to say that God caused these events, and that
entails for him the view that they cannot be explained by science. Tillich, on the other hand, wishes to say that such divine
interference cannot occur, and that God always works through
the known or unknown laws or structures of reality.

But just as Tillich asks the literalist how he can be so
sure that objective miracles occur, we must ask Tillich how he
can be so sure that they cannot. So far we have been led to
conclude that, for Tillich, an objective miracle is not to be
defined as a break in all known natural laws or as something
which cannot now be explained--for there are many things which
science today cannot explain, and surely we do not wish to call
them miracles. Thus we have considered a second alternative:

---

[69]S.T., II, pp. 103-104.

that for Tillich an objective miracle is something which in principle cannot be explained by reason or science in terms of natural laws. But I fear that this definition is also inadequate, for it is not Tillich's view. Tillich does not dogmatically claim that the forever unexplainable, or that which contradicts the structure of reality itself, cannot occur. Indeed, he thinks that such things do occur--as we have already seen in his comments about the "irrational," which he calls "an undeniable fact."[70] What he wishes to say is that if and when such things occur, they are not divine but demonic. The irrational and the objectively miraculous are similar in entailing a break in the structure of reality and therefore of human reason itself, but they differ in their purported source. Tillich accepts the irrational but rejects the objectively miraculous; this amounts to the view that if a break in the structure of reality occurred, it should not be called a miracle, since this suggests its origin in God. This is brought out clearly in Tillich's debate in Ultimate Concern. After being pressed as to why he is so sure that the law of gravity cannot be suspended, and after answering that the evidence is weak, etc., he finally responds to his persistent critics:

> But an actual negation of gravitation would not
> be for me a "miracle." If such a phenomenon
> occurred, it would be to me demonic, because it
> would deny the holy law by which all things in
> the universe strive toward each other. . . . The
> denial of this I would insist is a demonic form.[71]

And again, in the Systematic Theology he makes clear that he is not against the view that the structure of reality can be broken, but only that God can break this structure; indeed, Tillich is sure there are such demonic breaks:

> The supranaturalistic theory of miracles makes
> God a sorcerer and a cause of "possession"; it
> confuses God with demonic structures in the mind
> and reality. There are such structures, based on
> a distortion of genuine manifestations of the
> mystery of being.[72] (italics mine)

Here we finally seem to have received an answer from Tillich

---

[70]See above, p. 33.

[71]Brown, pp. 165-166. Cf. also his remarks about Jesus: "But if we consider the actions of Jesus during the storm in the Bible as affecting the whole meteorological constellation of the world, which this really would imply, then we would contribute to what I think is a demonic destruction of the structure of reality." (Ibid., p. 171)

[72]S.T., I, pp. 116-117.

as to what the term "objective miracle" means. It is not a break
in the known structure of reality, nor a break in all possible
structures of reality, but a break caused by God in all possible
structures of reality. One is believing in objective miracles
when one believes that events which are in principle rationally
unexplainable occur and are caused by God. It is this belief
that Tillich rejects when rejecting the belief in objective miracles as a "contradiction in terms,"[73] and this is why he states
with absolute certainty that "the manifestation of the mystery
of being [i.e., of God] does not destroy the structure of being
in which it becomes manifest."[74]

The belief in miracles is absurd because it involves
believing or accepting assertions which claim that God acts so
as to break the structures of reality--i.e., that God performs
acts which cannot be explained, acts which we must not even try
to explain. I believe that all Tillich's cases of absurdity,
even those not having to do with miracles, can be seen as cases
of ruling out questions. We might say that a belief is theologically absurd (as opposed to merely scientifically absurd) if
it involves believing something about God which demands giving
up the attempt to understand in terms of whatever rational categories we have.[75] Absurdity involves ceasing to question.
Tillich says that if God is considered to be literally omnipotent,
the question can be asked whether he could create a stone he
could not lift; the impossibility of answering such a question
shows "the absurdity to which you come if you persist in this
imagery."[76] If God is a highest being, he must ask himself, as
we do, where he came from;[77] the infinite regress could be

---

[73] S.T., I, p. 117.

[74] S.T., I, p. 115.

[75] Of course, Tillich does not think that we can ask all
questions about God. For example, we cannot ("properly") ask
why there is a God, or why there is anything, or Being (cf.
Rome, pp. 403-404). We must simply accept this. Presumably we
can, therefore, not ask why there is a structure of Being; the
rational man will see that the question itself makes no sense.
Particular things can be explained in terms of the structure of
Being (i.e., in terms of God as Logos), but to ask how the
structure of Being can be explained is to ask for another structure in terms of which to explain it.

[76] Brown, p. 170; cf. also S.T., I, pp. 273-274: "It is
magic and an absurdity if it is understood as the quality of a
highest being who is able to do what he wants."

[77] S.T., I, p. 196; cf. p. 209.

stopped only by the command to stop questioning. All views
which implicitly involve such a command are absurd. An ultimate
concern (i.e., a God) which demands that we not question is a
demonic ultimate concern and thus a false god.

We have made some progress. We have but one further question to ask of Tillich regarding absurdity, and then I believe
we will be able to see what he means by the protective function
of dogma. Suppose we meet somebody who is guilty of all the so-
called errors of supranaturalism, fundamentalism, and literalism.
Let us say he believes that every miracle in the Bible really
occurred, that every word in the Bible was dictated by God to its
writers, that Jesus ransomed our souls from the devil by dying
on the cross in our stead, and that all one has to do to be
assured of going to Heaven is to get oneself to believe these
things. However much we may disagree with him, why or when
should we not feel quite tolerant toward him? Why should we try
to get him to ask questions? Why not leave him alone, happy in
his faith and doctrine? Is it only because his unquestioning
expression of his faith (i.e., his interpretation of the Bible),
if it claims to be the only expression of the Christian faith,
turns the intellectuals away from Christianity and thus prevents
them from hearing the message? Is it only because, so to speak,
many intellectuals will simply not go to church if all churches
have fundamentalist pastors? Or is there a further, a non-
apologetic, reason? How is the church, and even the literalist
himself, endangered by the supposed command not to ask questions
about God and his works?

Tillich's answer is: consider the consequences. The literalist himself has to suppress his own reason; this leads to personal disintegration, fanaticism, hostility toward others, and
any number of other personal and communal forms of destruction.
Fundamentalism "has demonic traits. It destroys the humble honesty of the search for truth, it splits the conscience of its
thoughtful adherents, and it makes them fanatical because they
are forced to suppress elements of truth of which they are dimly
aware."[78] In theological theism, "God . . . deprives me of my
subjectivity because he is all-powerful and all-knowing. I
revolt and try to make him into an object, but the revolt fails
and becomes desperate. . . . This is the God Nietzsche said had
to be killed."[79] "Some forms of fundamentalism are a soul-

---

[78] S.T., I, p. 3.

[79] The Courage to Be, p. 185.

42

destroying demonization of Christianity, because they foster dishonesty."[80] Literalism "is unjustifiable if a mature mind is
broken in its personal center by political or psychological
methods, split in his unity, and hurt in his integrity."[81] Dogma
should be "interpreted in such a way that it is no longer a sup-
pressive power which produces dishonesty or flight."[82] Reducing
the work of the Spirit to establishing a conviction of the literal truth of the biblical words "contradicts the nature of the
Spirit and therefore amounts to a security-seeking surrender to
authority."[83] "Demonic suppression of honest obedience to the
structures of truth is at stake here."[84]

The point of all this is to show that for Tillich dogma does
not protect against falsehood or incorrect belief, but against
demonic or destructive consequences. Absurdity is objectionable
in theology not because absurd beliefs are false, not because
absurd beliefs are theoretically incorrect interpretations of
what Bible or tradition "really" meant, but because absurd
beliefs are destructive. Dogma gives practical protection, not
theoretical protection. Theological and religious assertions
are symbolic, and thus not subject to abstract questions of
truth:

> Symbolic statements about God, his attributes,
> and his actions are not false or correct, but
> they are "demonic" or "divine," and in most
> cases they are mixed (ambiguous). The criter-
> ion is whether their implications are destruc-
> tive or creative for personality and community.[85]
> (italics mine)

A theological assertion is not true in the sense of truly
descriptive of God in himself; it is true insofar as it properly
judges the effects and consequences of ordinary religious sym-

---

[80]Brown, p. 24. Tillich uses the case of a boy's deification of his mother to illustrate his point that the deification
of something finite is not just false but destructive.

[81]Dynamics of Faith, p. 53.

[82]A History of Christian Thought, p. xvi.

[83]S.T., III, p. 128. Tillich's attack upon the belief that
revelation is information is generally due to his conviction
that such an idea leads to dishonesty and suppression (S.T., I,
p. 129).

[84]S.T., III, p. 106; cf. also p. 174: No one can "honestly
carry" such a burden.

[85]Rome, p. 387.

bols.[86] It is true in a pragmatic sense.[87] Idolatrous faith,
in which the Bible or any other finite reality is made into one's
"God" or ultimate concern, is not false but destructive--or, better, to say that it is false is to say that it is destructive.

> The inescapable consequence of idolatrous
> faith is "existential disappointment". .
> . . The ecstatic character of even an idola-
> trous faith can hide this consequence only
> for a certain time. But finally it breaks
> out into the open.[88]

Thus Tillich judges the tree by its fruits.[89] If one asks
what consequences literalism or supranaturalism has besides those
of offending the cultured, i.e., if one asks what right have the
cultured to be offended, Tillich answers that they have a divine
right, precisely because they see the demonic consequences of
absurdity.

Does this mean, then, that Tillich applies the protective
criterion against literalism only when it leads to personal and
communal disintegration? Indeed it does mean this; there is no
question of absolute truth here, but only of consequences. "What
one can and should do is to 'deliteralize' them [i.e., symbols]
for those who are able and willing to apply rational criteria to
the meaning of religious symbols."[90] (italics mine) Again,
Tillich points out that we must distinguish two stages of literalism, the natural and the reactive. The first stage is that
in which the mythical and the literal are not distinguished, and
"this stage has a full right of its own and should not be dis-
turbed, . . . up to the moment when man's questioning mind
breaks the natural acceptance of the mythological visions as
literal."[91] At this point many people "who prefer the repression
of their questions to the uncertainty which appears with the
breaking of myth" will be forced into reactive or conscious lit-

---

[86]Ibid., p. 390.

[87]Ibid., p. 393. Tillich notes that he accepts an existential, not scientific (detached) pragmatism. The risk of faith
is not merely cognitive.

[88]Dynamics of Faith, p. 12.

[89]Tillich accepts Luther's Christology, which is based on
Christ's effects or benefits (A History of Christian Thought,
p. 249; S.T., II, p. 168).

[90]S.T., III, p. 142.

[91]Dynamics of Faith, p. 52.

eralism.[92] This is what is bad, for it leads to the splitting
of one's personal center. "The enemy of a critical theology is
not natural literalism but conscious literalism with repression
of and aggression toward autonomous thought."[93]

To put this point more strongly, Tillich does not seem to
be saying that it is "in fact" false that God performs objective
miracles. Who knows whether "in fact" he does or not? We have
no direct knowledge of God or being-itself; we have no knowledge
of the way things really are, independently of all human minds.
The belief in objective miracles is not absolutely false; it is
destructive.

Once we have seen the fundamental thrust of Tillich's
attack on literalism, it is easy to generalize our results. One
of the most common kinds of argument Tillich uses against any
theological position or assertion is that its consequences are
destructive. Doctrine attempts to protect against dangerous
consequences. The concept of predestination protects against
"both human incertitude and human arrogance."[94] The consequences
of naturalism are "resignation or cynicism."[95] Luther's doctrine
of sola gratia was due to his experience that if salvation is
not solely the result of God's grace, the consequence is des-
pair.[96] The consequence of a non-paradoxical view of providence
is that "faith in providence breaks down, taking with it faith
in God and in the meaning of life and of history. Much cynicism
is the result of an erroneous and therefore disappointed confidence in individual or historical providence."[97]

---

[92]Ibid., pp. 52-53.

[93]Ibid., p. 53. Tillich makes the same point in Ultimate
Concern (Brown, pp. 193-195). He says that in his preaching he
tries not to give directly negative statements against literalism, but if people ask, he answers. Not literalism but the
destructive repression of natural questions is what is bad:
"The worst thing, and I censure them sincerely, is the reply of
some Sunday-school teachers, when children ask questions: 'You
must not ask, you must believe.' My reaction to that is very
barbaric: I would say, 'Throw those teachers out tomorrow morn-
ing! Forever!'"

[94]S.T., I, p. 285.

[95]S.T., II, p. 30.

[96]A History of Christian Thought, p. 236.

[97]S.T., I, pp. 268-269; cf. also Brown, pp. 123-124, where
Tillich says that whereas the consequence of utopianism is that
the meaning of life breaks down when the utopia does not occur
(interestingly, he calls this metaphysical as opposed to psychological disappointment), the consequence of other-worldliness is

In general, then, one gets the strong feeling that for
Tillich a doctrine's "truth" is determined by its consequences.
Indeed, he often judges the value of certain ways of speaking by
their effects even if the intent was to avoid such effects. For
example, Luther's intent in expressing himself in terms of the
doctrine of "justification by faith" was correct, and yet the
expression must be rejected because it tends to be misinterpreted
to mean that justification involves believing the right things,
and this leads simply to disastrous results (and the exact opposite of what Luther intended).[98] He suggests that calling the
Bible the Word of God, while perhaps the intention can be and
sometimes is correct, nevertheless is often misunderstood, leading
for example to dishonesty.[99] He criticizes Schleiermacher's use
of the word "feeling" because it led people to misunderstand what
Schleiermacher was getting at, and this in turn often had the
consequence of making religion sentimental and weak.[100]

In all this, of course, there is an obvious dialectic
between the apologetic and the protective aims of dogma. In general a doctrine that is apologetically offensive will also be
dangerous to members of the church, and vice versa. The person
who is offended acts on the basis of a criterion which serves
to protect against dangerous consequences. Schleiermacher's use
of the term "feeling," according to Tillich, not only led to the
weakening of the faith of certain Christians, but also to a
rejection of the faith by those who wanted sharp thought and
moral significance."[101] In both cases, a misunderstanding of
Schleiermacher's intent was at stake, but Schleiermacher's words
had a life of their own, so to speak: they tended to be misunderstood. Tillich's point is that no matter how carefully our
words are defined, their connotations (whence they derive most

---

the abandonment of the world and its problems to hell. For
Tillich's struggle with the question of utopianism, see especially A History of Christian Thought, pp. 119-120, where he con-
cludes that he speaks out against utopianism even though this
may cause a weakening of efforts at social reform; thus he calls
his stance "a very questionable" decision.

[98] S.T., II, pp. 85, 179.

[99] S.T., I, p. 158.

[100] Perspectives on Nineteenth and Twentieth Century Protestant Theology, ed. Carl E. Braaten (New York: Harper and Row,
1967), pp. 97-98.

[101] Ibid., p. 98.

of their power) are not under our control.

This would seem to mean that much theological activity must involve an effort to see what consequences the use of certain words and doctrines have had in the past. Of course, there is always a risk involved, but we can predict "inductively" the probable or possible consequences of specific formulations. Tillich often argues that "history shows" that the consequences of a given doctrine are of a certain type. He criticizes, for example, the various ways of self-salvation,[102] Buber's opposition to political Zionism,[103] popular existentialism,[104] Thomas Aquinas' "cosmological" approach to religion,[105] and many other views by claiming that history shows that they have certain dangerous consequences. Indeed, he even indicates that he judged his own early philosophical and theological positions on the basis of their effects:

> If Hitler is the outcome of what we believed
> to be the true philosophy and the only theology,
> both must be false. With this rather desperate
> conclusion we left Germany.[106]

I do not intend to analyze all the various kinds of consequences against which dogma, and theology in general, should protect. But perhaps a word regarding Tillich's general point of view would be helpful. According to Tillich, the two fundamental dangers of religion are demonization (or idolatry) and profanization (or secularization).

> The first ambiguity of religion is that of
> self-transcendence and profanization in the

---

[102]S.T., II, pp. 81-86.

[103]Theology of Culture, p. 199.

[104]The Courage to Be, p. 146.

[105]A History of Christian Thought, p. 186; Theology of Culture, p. 26.

[106]Theology of Culture, p. 164. All this can be related, I believe, to Tillich's view that the past can change; it can become something different, depending upon its eventual consequences. It can "change its aspect." Tillich's eschatology also makes use of this idea. The past is not ontologically static, and thus even it can be "saved." "For God the past is not complete, because through it he creates the future; and in creating the future, he re-creates the past. If the past were only the sum total of what happened, such an assertion would be meaningless. But the past includes its own potentialities. . . . The past becomes something different through everything new which happens. Its aspects change" (S.T., I, p. 276). What Tillich here calls potentialities are related to what we have been calling consequences (potential consequences can become actual consequences).

religious function itself. The second ambiguity
of religion is the demonic elevation of something conditioned to unconditional validity. One
can say that religion always moves between the
danger points of profanization and demonization,
and that in every genuine act of the religious
life both are present, openly or covertly.[107]

Profanization is the process of transforming religion into
a finite object among finite objects. Its fundamental characteristic is the absence or reduction of <u>power</u>; it is empty or life-
less or weak. Thus religious symbols can be judged, in part, by
their "adequacy of expression."

> Faith has truth in so far as it adequately
> expresses an ultimate concern. "Adequacy" of
> expression means the power of expressing an
> ultimate concern in such a way that it creates
> reply, action, communication. Symbols which
> are able to do this are alive. But the life
> of symbols is limited. . . . A divine figure
> ceases to create reply, it ceases to be a com-
> mon symbol and loses its power to move for
> action. . . . If we look from this point of
> view at the history of faith, including our
> own period, the criterion of truth is whether
> or not it is alive. This, certainly, is not
> an exact criterion in any scientific sense,
> but it is a pragmatic one that can be applied
> rather easily to the past with its streams of
> obviously dead symbols.[108]

The other danger of faith is demonic or idolatrous distortion. "The demonic does not resist self-transcendence as does
the profane, but it distorts self-transcendence by identifying
a particular bearer of holiness with the holy itself."[109] The
demonic engenders estrangement, division, conflict, <u>splitness</u>.

> A main characteristic of the demonic is the
> state of being split. This is easily under-
> standable on the basis of the demonic's claim
> to divinity on a finite basis: the elevation
> of one element of finitude to infinite power
> and meaning necessarily produces the reaction
> from other elements of finitude, which deny
> such a claim or make it for themselves.[110]

And thus we have another criterion with which to judge religious
symbols:

> The other criterion of the truth of a symbol of
> faith is that it expresses the ultimate which is
> really ultimate. In other words, that it is not

---

[107]<u>S.T.</u>, III, p. 98. Cf. also Brown, p. 5.

[108]<u>Dynamics of Faith</u>, pp. 96-97.

[109]<u>S.T.</u>, III, p. 102.

[110]<u>Ibid.</u>, p. 103.

> idolatrous. . . . Every type of faith has the
> tendency to elevate its concrete symbols to
> absolute validity. The criterion of the truth
> of faith, therefore, is that it implies an
> element of self-negation. That symbol is most
> adequate which expresses not only the ultimate
> but its own lack of ultimacy.[111]

In general, we can see Tillich's criticisms of particular
types of faith or theology as directed predominantly toward
either their profaning or their demonizing tendencies. Tillich
most commonly charges naturalism, humanism, and theological liberalism with powerlessness,[112] and he most often accuses supranaturalism, neo-orthodoxy, and fundamentalism with such expressions of the demonic as fanaticism, suppression of truth, and
personal and communal disintegration.[113] The ideal type of faith
would thus be one which is both _holy_ (non-profane) and _divine_
(non-demonic);[114] it would possess _power_ as well as _rational_
self-criticism. The two fundamental elements in God's manifestation, his character as power and as _logos_, would be united;
the concretely actualized unity of these is the work of God's
Spirit (or of God _as_ Spirit).[115]

As an example of the dialectics of the profane and the
demonic, we can refer to our above analysis of absurdity.
Absurdity in theology leads to demonic splits: it splits the
individual from himself (i.e., from his own reason) and from
other men; it is the result of denying the _logos_ character of
God. It leads to personal disintegration and to fanaticism. But
it also leads to a profanizing of religion: for those who cannot accept the absurdities (or dangerous consequences) of pas-
sionate literalism, the result is either a weak and insincere

---

[111] _Dynamics of Faith_, p. 97.

[112] Cf., for example, _S.T._, I, p. 154; II, pp. 106, 152; III,
p. 348; _Dynamics of Faith_, p. 64.

[113] Here we need only refer to Tillich's analysis of literalism and absurdity. Interestingly, Tillich claims that mono-
theism leads to emptiness, while polytheism leads to demonic
splits. Does this mean that supranaturalism (e.g. Barthian neo-
orthodoxy) is not monotheistic? Yes, strangely enough. Tillich
claims that it leads to a dualism like that of the Manichaean
and Marcionite heresies (_S.T._, I, p. 155; _A History of Christian
Thought_, pp. 34, 44).

[114] Cf. _S.T._, III, pp. 98-106, where Tillich suggests this
distinction between the holy and the divine. Cf. also _S.T._, I,
pp. 215-216, where he says that the demonic is still "holy."
It has holy power but is antidivine.

[115] _S.T._, I, pp. 250-251.

faith or else, as for the alienated intellectuals, no faith at
all and a resultant subjectivism, resignation, and cynicism. And
then "a vacuum is produced, into which distorted reason can break
without rational check."[116] Thus profanization and demonization
give birth to one another. The over-exaggerations of the one
lead to the over-exaggerations of the other, and one need only
choose whether to be destroyed by Scylla or by Charybdis.

Thus everything depends upon keeping the "ontological elements" in proper balance, for these elements are present in
Being itself or in God himself.[117] The demonic splitting of
individuation from participation, of dynamics from form, and of
freedom from destiny leads to destruction. An overemphasis upon
the individual, upon dynamics, and upon freedom leads to chaos;
whereas an overemphasis upon participation, upon form, and upon
destiny leads to emptiness.[118]

Thus on the basis of our examination of Tillich's concept
of dogma, we can say that theology, the "logos of theos," or
rational thought about God (as he is given to us in faith), has
a double function. It has an apologetic function insofar as it
tries to formulate the Christian faith in terms acceptable to
the intellectuals. Thus two of the most "theoretical" elements
in Tillich's thought, his use of ontological language and his
attempts to avoid absurdity, have been shown to have partly apologetic aims. But theology also has a protective function: its
doctrines attempt to protect against certain dangerous practical

---

[116]Ibid., p. 93.

[117]Cf. S.T., I, pp. 174-186, for Tillich's discussion of
the three pairs of ontological elements.

[118]The best example of this point is Tillich's various discussions of ecstasy. Ecstasy is necessary; else religion
becomes weak and empty. But ecstasy must be united with structure; also "existential disappointment" ensues, as in intoxication or the various spirit-movements. The mark of subjective
ecstasy (or "intoxication") is that, while temporarily satisfying,
it is destructive "in the long run"; it is, in a sense, self-
contradictory, for it heightens "the tensions it wants to avoid"
(S.T., III, p. 119). Without ecstasy, there is profanization;
without structure, demonization (Ibid., pp. 116-117; cf. also
S.T., I, pp. 113-115). Many people see the excesses of the
ecstatic movements and over-react by rejecting ecstasy as such;
spirit-movements see the excesses of this over-reaction and again
over-react by rejecting structure and rationality. In the
absence of the Spirit, or the unity of both sides, the divine
becomes profaned and the holy becomes demonic. In this sense,
Tillich's theology is based upon the doctrine of the Holy Spirit.
Without the Spiritual Presence man's encounter with Being (or
God) is destructive: God is either "burning fire" or sheer
emptiness (S.T., I, pp. 250-251).

consequences. We have seen that absurdity is by no means a merely theoretical issue for Tillich, nor is it solely an apologetic issue. Those who accept absurdities are themselves in danger. But what about ontological language? Does it, too, have a protective role? Is the church itself in danger if it rejects ontology? It is to this question that we now turn.

A. Two Types of Faith

We have considered two main reasons for the use of dogma
and rational thought in theology, but now we must return to our
problem of the use of the rather strange kind of rational thought
which uses ontological concepts such as being, essence, and participation. We have already seen that one reason for the use of
such language is an apologetic one. Can we find any other reason? It might be thought that another reason follows directly
from the fact that literalism has to be rejected. After all,
does not something have to fill the vacuum left by the rejection
of literalism? If Tillich is right that literalism is bad in
theology (for both apologetic and protective reasons), then perhaps theology must reject a literal interpretation of religious
language and as a replacement use an ontological or a philosophical language, in which literal statements which are not absurd
can be made. But there would be several objections to this justification of ontology even if Tillich used it. In the first
place, one could ask why any language must replace literalism?
Why not keep the original religious language and merely point
out that it is to be understood symbolically and not literally?
This would avoid the absurdities of literalism; one could still
say "God created the world," so long as one understood that such
language is not literal, i.e., that it is not "information," but
is the expression of one quality of a certain kind of experience
or awareness. The words have the right "feel" or "sound"; they
seem appropriate, and become inappropriate only if taken liter-
ally--for they were not (or should not have been) intended literally. One would not here have to give an ontological interpretation of the words in terms of being, non-being, essence,
and so on.

But in the second place, it would be quite contrary to
Tillich to suggest that ontology gives the correct interpretation of symbolic religious language, i.e., that it is the
replacement of an absurd literalistic understanding of religious
language with a non-absurd literalistic understanding. For
ontology, too, according to Tillich, becomes symbolic when used
in theology. Although in its own sphere it strives to use lit-

51

eral language just as science does, when such concepts are used
to apply to the divine they become symbolic. We do not learn or
say something about God himself by using ontological language,
we only express something; and if this expression is understood
to apply adequately, in the sense of literally, to God, then it
becomes quite as objectionable as any other literalistic language
when applied to God[1] (though perhaps objectionable for different
reasons--i.e., it may not be demonic but powerless).

But if this is so, the question must recur: why ontology
in theology? That is, what non-apologetic reason might there be
to give a positive evaluation of a theology which uses ontological concepts and a negative evaluation of one which radically
rejects them? Might there be a protective reason for the use of
ontology as well as an apologetic one?

We have already seen that Tillich often suggests that ontology must be used because it is implicit in ordinary religious
discourse; indeed, most of Tillich's little book, Biblical Religion and the Search for Ultimate Reality,[2] is the attempt to
show this. But what could it mean that ontology is somehow implicit in biblical religion? And even if such a claim could be
clarified and then substantiated, what (non-apologetic) reason
could the church have for desiring to make the ontology explicit?
Further, Tillich often justifies his use of ontology by referring to the fact that many classical theologians of a certain
variety have emphasized such language. But again, what was their
reason for using it, and what reason does the church today have
for following their lead?

Tillich often responds to those who criticize his use of
ontology by claiming that even his critics use ontological concepts, whether they know it or not.[3] The suggestion here is
that some kind of ontology is presupposed in virtually any kind
of discourse, and thus the question is not so much whether to
have an ontology, but whether to have a good or bad ontology.
Here, of course, the concept of ontology is used in its very
broadest sense, according to which even nominalism and logical

---

[1]Cf. Tillich's replies to Hartshorne and Bertocci in Rome,
pp. 376-378, where he makes clear that to speak literally of God
is to make God finite and thus no longer God. ("A 'finite God'
is a contradiction in terms," p. 376). Tillich will no more
accept Hartshorne's highly philosophical literalism than he will
accept biblical literalism.

[2]Chicago: The University of Chicago Press, 1955.

[3]S.T., I, pp. 19-20, 230-231; Kegley and Bretall, p. 343.

positivism have an ontology,[4] and the term "ontology" is more or
less equated with "presuppositions about reality." With the problem of this concept of ontology we shall deal in the last chapter; it shall prove our hardest nut to crack. In this chapter
we shall be concerned with what Tillich's critics are perhaps
getting at, namely why Tillich chooses this particular brand of
ontology   order to express himself. The ontology he uses is
obviously heavily indebted to idealism and mysticism or, more
accurately, to that kind of idealism which includes a strong element of mysticism, best represented by such philosophers as Plato,
Plotinus, Spinoza, Hegel, and especially Schelling. Whatever
else one says about this type of ontology, one can say in the
first place that it is most difficult ɔ understand, and in the
second place that it seems to fit rather poorly with (and perhaps
openly conflict with) the "ontology" presupposed in Scripture.
No doubt Tillich's type of ontology may be apologetically valuable, as we saw in the first chapter; some intellectuals will be
more open to a message expressed in idealistic language than to
one expressed in the language of the Bible. But is there a further reason to use such language? Why did Tillich not choose a
"simpler" ontology with which to correct the excesses of supranaturalism? Why did he not express himself without the use of
abstract idealistic and rationalistic terminology?

I wish to put forward a suggestion which I think goes some
way, though not all the way, toward answering these questions.
To state it concisely, I believe that Tillich sees classical
ontological language as, to some extent, an expression of one of
the two major types of faith in the Christian tradition. Ontological language is the language of the ontological or mystical
type of faith,[5] as opposed to the more personalistic, nominalistic, or legalistic kind of language which expresses the moral or
prophetic type of faith. Tillich's view is that each type of
faith has a dialectical dependence upon the other; they are polar

---

[4] S.T., I, pp. 20, 230-231.

[5] Or, perhaps more accurately, the conceptualization of the
language of mysticism. For example, ordinary mystical language
might speak symbolically of God as the ocean or the light; a
more conceptualized language prefers to speak of God as the
power of being or as Being itself. The reason for conceptualizing mystical language might be the same as the reason for conceptualizing prophetic language: to protect against literalistic distortion (God is not literally an ocean just as he is not
literally a father). I am not, however, aware of passages where
Tillich warns against literalistic distortions of mystical language. Perhaps for some reason there is less danger of it in
mysticism.

types of faith *each* of which suffers if its opposite is omitted or down-played. That is, they are *essentially* unified and whenever they are separated, faith becomes endangered: the consequences are dangerous (demonic or profane). For various historical reasons, such as today's nominalistic way of thinking and the upsurge of a strong overemphasis upon the prophetic, judgmental type of faith under the leadership of Barth and other crisis theologians, our age is in special danger of distorting faith by separating it from its mystical side. Thus Tillich wishes to correct the balance, so to speak, by expressing this side of faith, utilizing for this purpose the language which traditionally has best expressed it, namely, ontological language. Our task now is to substantiate this suggestion.

To begin with, we can note that the ontological-prophetic distinction recurs again and again in one form or another throughout Tillich's works. Many, if not most, of his distinctions between kinds of faith, religion, theology, and even philosophy of religion are reducible to this distinction.[6] In Tillich's later writings, the distinction is most clearly made in Dynamics of Faith, where Tillich states that there are "two main elements in every experience of the holy."[7] The first is the experience of the holiness of being, the presence of the holy here and now. The holy "grasps the mind with terrifying and fascinating power."[8] The second is the experience of the holiness of what ought to be; it demands justice and love. Here the holy stands as "the judgment over everything that is."[9] Corresponding to these two elements of the experience of the holy, there are two types of faith, depending upon which element predominates. The first Tillich calls the ontological type of faith, and the second the moral type of faith. "The dynamics of faith within and between the religions are largely determined by these two types, their interdependence and their conflict."[10] The two elements are

---

[6]With the exception of secularism or humanism, which however is not properly a religion but a quasi-religion. Or, one could say that it is the secularization of one of the two types of faith. Cf. Dynamics of Faith, p. 64, where Tillich distinguishes the ontological and the moral types of humanist faith, the former being "romantic-conservative," the latter "progressive-utopian."

[7]Dynamics of Faith, p. 56.

[8]Ibid., p. 56.

[9]Ibid., p. 56.

[10]Ibid., pp. 56-57. Cf. also A History of Christian Thought, where Tillich at several points refers to one or both of these

present in every act of faith, and yet one always predominates because of man's finitude, preventing him from ever uniting all elements of truth in complete balance. The ontological type of faith is mainly represented by sacramentalism and mysticism.[11] These two are related, but mystical faith, instead of seeing the holy in something concrete, transcends every concrete reality. Or, we might say, in mysticism the holy is found not in any external objects but in the depths of the human soul, "the point of contact between the finite and the infinite."[12]

The second type of faith, the moral, is also subdivided into several kinds, of which the most significant is that represented by the Jewish prophets and Old Testament Judaism in general.[13] Moral obedience rather than rituals or asceticism is especially demanded. "The world historical mission of the Jewish faith is to judge the sacramental self-certainty in Judaism itself, as well as in all other religions, and to pronouce an ultimate concern which denies any claim for ultimacy that does not include the demand of justice."[14]

Tillich then goes on to state two things that will be of great importance for our analysis. In the first place, he says that although the moral type of faith is present in ancient Greek humanism and philosophy, nevertheless "the ontological type remained predominant in all ancient history. The victory of mysticism in Greek philosophy and of the mystery religions in the Roman Empire, the lack of progressive and utopian thinking in the sphere of antiquity prove it."[15] Thus in the western world the Greeks are especially representative of the ontological or mystical type of faith, just as the Old Testament Jews are especially representative of the moral type.

In the second place, Tillich emphasizes again that the

_____

types. For example, he distinguishes between Augustine's "mystical-ontological" thinking and his "ethical-educational thinking" (pp. 119-120).

[11]Dynamics of Faith, pp. 58-62. In other places Tillich considers sacramentalism to be the fundamental type of faith, while mysticism and prophetism are the two religious ways of correcting its excesses. Cf. S.T., I, pp. 139-142; The Future of Religions, ed. Jerald C. Brauer (New York: Harper and Row, 1966), pp. 81, 86-87.

[12]Dynamics of Faith, p. 61.

[13]Ibid., pp. 65-68.

[14]Ibid., p. 68.

[15]Ibid.

types of faith are essentially united and that any type of faith
must, in order to be faith at all, have some element of its opposite.[16] But especially interesting are Tillich's remarks on
Christianity here. The Christian theologian, he says, "will see
in Christianity--and especially Protestant Christianity--the aim
toward which the dynamics of faith are driving."[17] That is, the
Christian theologian will try to show that Christianity embodies
in a particularly sensitive way the proper union of the types of
faith. The New Testament "represents a union of ethical and
mystical types." Tillich says that Paul's doctrine of the Spirit
is a good example: "Faith, in the New Testament, is the state
of being grasped by the divine Spirit. As _Spirit_ it is the presence of the divine power in the human mind; as _holy_ Spirit it
is the spirit of love, justice, and truth."[18]

We must note what all this may mean for us. Does not
Tillich suggest that Christianity might be seen as, in a sense,
a fusion (synthesis) of the Greek and Jewish types of faith? Or
if this is too strong, can we not infer from Tillich's remarks
that, given the fact that Christianity is a fusion of the ontological and moral types of faith (however much or little this
can be traced to its Jewish and Greek ancestry), the legalistic
language of the prophets might best express its moral side while
the philosophical (ontological) language of the Greeks might best
express its _mystical_ side? Might we not say that, insofar as
Christianity has a stronger emphasis upon the ontological side
than Judaism did, the concepts of the Old Testament would not
easily be able to express this side with its proper emphasis--

---

[16]_Ibid._, pp. 69-70.

[17]_Ibid._, pp. 70-71.

[18]_Ibid._, p. 71. It may be of interest to compare Tillich's
idea of the polarity between the holiness of what is and the
holiness of what ought to be to what he considers to be two
meanings of the term "essence," the descriptive and the evalua-
tive (_S.T._, I, pp. 202-203). According to the former, the
essence of something is what it essentially _is_, or that which
makes it what it is (in the sense of _defining_ it); in the latter,
essence is what something essentially _ought to be_, as opposed
to what it is. In the first case essence is seen as the _power_
of being; in the second, as the _judgement_ over being. Tillich
notes that these two "meanings" of essence are united in princi-
p-e (i.e., essentially!); it is only due to man's estrangement
in existence that what ought to be is not what is. In existence,
therefore, those who see man as united with being and those who
see man as separated from being, each emphasize one side to the
exclusion of the other; the former is obviously more appropriate
to ontological types of faith and the latter to moral types.

and that Greek philosophical language might better do the job?

That this is the case can, I believe, be substantiated by considering the similarity between Tillich's concepts of mysticism and ontology. Perhaps we can best see this by considering some other places where variations of the fundamental distinction between the ontological and the moral types of faith recur.

B. Mysticism and Ontology

Some such distinction between two types of faith or between two elements in every kind of faith is found throughout Tillich's writings. It would be an enormous task to show in detail the extent to which Tillich's many distinctions between types of faith or of philosophy or of theology can be understood in the light of this fundamental distinction. Above all, we would be confronted with the fact that Tillich either changed his mind regarding the value and extent of mysticism in religion or else used the term "mystical" in several ways. Sometimes Tillich uses the word "mystical" to refer to any experience of God, in which case sacramentalism and nearly any living faith would somehow be mystically oriented; sometimes he uses the term to refer to the "abstract" mysticism which abstracts from any content and is thus to be distinguished from sacramentalism and yet seen as a development, partly dependent upon it and partly critical of it, beyond sacramentalism; and sometimes he uses the term to refer to a third possibility: a concrete mysticism, or a mysticism of love, (or, again, a "Christ-mysticism") which returns to earth, so to speak, and includes within itself the prophetic demands for justice and attention to this world. All this can be incredibly confusing, and the confusion is compounded by the fact that ontology, which we would like to compare to mysticism, is also understood by Tillich in various ways (perhaps one way for each kind of mysticism).

But if we are to avoid writing the several volumes which it would take to straighten out all these ambiguities, we must not get too involved in the intricacies of the matter but must, rather, stand at a distance to see certain obvious patterns. And the fundamental pattern in Tillich's thought rests on a more-or-less clear distinction: between that type of faith which speaks of God as sheer being (or essence or substance), which tends therefore to be pantheistic, which emphasizes participation, the "vertical" line, eternity as timelessness, and so on, as opposed to that type of faith which speaks of God as a personal, highest being, which is theistic, which tends to emphasize individuality, the "horizontal" line, and eternity as endless time. The first

type is the "ontological" type; it stresses <u>union</u>. The second
type is the "moral" type; it emphasizes separation and <u>judgment</u>.
The question of how to re-unite these types of faith which are in
principle united but have become separated, re-uniting them on a
higher level than that which constituted their original union
(i.e., uniting them not as in the original stage of "dreaming
innocence" but as in the eschatological stage of love) is
Tillich's basic problem: it makes for the triadic character of
his theology centering upon the concepts of Creation, Fall, and
Salvation (or union, separation, and re-union). Salvation <u>is</u> a
possibility, for Tillich, but it must not involve a simple return
to Paradise (thus making meaningless man's Fall, all his suffer-
ings, and the temporal world in general); rather, it must make
sense even of pain, suffering, and evil at the same time that
the tragic (and genuinely evil) character of evil is admitted.

But again the sympathetic reader will permit me, perhaps to
avoid attempting to lay out the whole of Tillich's theology. We
are fundamentally concerned with Tillich's idea that there are,
broadly speaking, two elements in faith or two types of faith.
Let us observe some of the other contexts in which such a distinction emerges.

In <u>The Courage to Be</u>, Tillich draws a distinction between
two kinds of courage: the courage to be as a part and the courage to be as oneself. The courage to be as oneself is "the
affirmation of the self as a self; that is of a separated, self-
centered, individualized, incomparable, free, self-determining
self."[19] The courage to be as a part is the affirmation of that
in which we participate--e.g., a group or a movement.[20] Each of
these can be considered a kind of courage, and each can be considered a kind of anxiety.[21] Thus in individualism the courage
to be as oneself and the anxiety about losing oneself in the
collective predominate,[22] while in collectivism and conformism
the courage to be as a part and the anxiety about losing one's
world predominate.[23] What is relevant to us in this distinction
is that Tillich applies it to two kinds of religion or religious
experience. The kind which emphasizes participation is <u>mysticism</u>.

---

[19]<u>The Courage to Be</u>, p. 86.

[20]<u>Ibid</u>., p. 89.

[21]<u>Ibid</u>., p. 90.

[22]<u>Ibid</u>., chapter 5.

[23]<u>Ibid</u>., chapter 4.

"In mysticism the individual self strives for a participation in the ground of being which approaches identification."[24] The mystic affirms his _essential_ self and negates as illusory all that, in himself and the world, which is finite. "Since being in time and space and under the categories of finitude is ultimately unreal, the vicissitudes arising from it and the final non-being ending it are equally unreal."[25]

The other kind of religion or religious experience is that which emphasizes individuation or the courage to be as oneself. Tillich calls it the type of the personal or divine-human encounter.[26] God is encountered or experienced as personal.

> Theism in this sense emphasizes the personalistic passages in the Bible and the Protestant creeds, the personalistic image of God, the word as the tool of creation and revelation, the ethical and social character of the kingdom of God, the personal nature of human faith and divine forgiveness, the historical vision of the universe, the idea of a divine purpose, the infinite distance between creator and created, the absolute separation between God and the world, the conflict between holy God and sinful man, the person-to-person character of prayer and practical devotion. Theism in this sense is the non-mystical side of biblical religion and historical Christianity.[27]

Both these types of relationship to God are valid, for Tillich, but both must be transcended because they are one-sided.[28] Real faith "embraces both mystical participation and personal confidence."[29] The great religious personalities of the past, though they inevitably emphasized one side or the other, were always aware of the other side. Insofar as we omit one side in conceptualizing our experience, our resultant philosophy or theology is deficient and even dangerous. However valuable the views based on mystical participation may be, they inevitably overlook the reality of this world, especially man's

---

[24]_Ibid._, p. 157. Tillich notes that Spinoza's system has a mystical background.

[25]_Ibid._, p. 158.

[26]_Ibid._, pp. 156, 160ff. He refuses to call it _faith_, insofar as it lacks the element of participation; similarly, he does not here consider mysticism to be faith unless it has the element of individuation (cf. pp. 156-157). But this is a small semantic point.

[27]_Ibid._, p. 183.

[28]_Ibid._, pp. 184, 186.

[29]_Ibid._, p. 160.

freedom and man's estrangement,[30] while a theology which conceptualizes the divine-human encounter, without any element of mystical participation, makes God into a being who, if he exists at
all, is a tyrant.[31] Both views are contrary to the Christian
view of God.

What is interesting here is the extent to which Tillich sees
the ontologies of such men as Socrates, Plato, the Stoics, the
Neoplatonists, Spinoza, and even Hegel and Heidegger, as arising
from the mystical type of faith.[32] Their religious roots are
often hard to detect, but they basically emphasize salvation
through participation. But it is precisely these philosophers
who use the kind of ontological language which Tillich himself
uses. In other words, there seems to be a close relation between
mysticism and Tillich's kind of ontological language. It is a
realistic (or idealistic or naturalistic) ontological language,
rather than a nominalistic one.

In his lectures on Nineteenth and Twentieth Century Protestant Thought, Tillich makes continual use of a distinction
similar to the one between the two types of faith. In discussing the eighteenth century conflicts between theological naturalism (or rationalism) and supranaturalism, he points out that
there is a close relation between rationalism and mysticism.

> Rationalism and mysticism do not stand in con-
> trast to each other, as is so often thought.
> Both in Greek and modern culture rationalism
> is the daughter of mysticism. Rationalism
> developed out of the mystical experience of
> the "inner light" or of the "inner truth" in
> every human being. Reason emerged within us
> out of mystical experiences, namely, the
> experience of the divine presence within us.
> . . . The opposite of a theology of inwardness
> is the classical theology of the Reformers,
> namely, the theology of the Word of God which
> comes to us from the outside, stands over
> against us and judges us, so that we have to
> accept it on the authority of the revelatory
> experience of the prophets and apostles. This
> whole conflict is of fundamental importance to
> the movements of theology in the centuries that
> we wish to discuss.[33]

---

[30]Ibid., pp. 169-170.

[31]Ibid., pp. 184-185.

[32]Ibid., pp. 23, 125, 133-135, 149, 157, 168-170.

[33]Nineteenth and Twentieth Century Protestant Thought, p.
19. Cf. also pp. 21-22, 45, 72, 78, 82, where Tillich repeats
the idea that rationalism arises from mysticism. In A History
of Christian Thought, he makes the same point again (p. 286).
For the importance, for Tillich, of transcending the split

Tillich goes on to note that this conflict is not only at the root of the struggle between German classical idealism and the rebirth of orthodoxy in the nineteenth century, but also between his own theology and Karl Barth's in our day.[34] He admits that he himself inclines toward the side of experience and inwardness,[35] though in principle he believes that the dispute between himself and Barth can be healed on the basis of Paul's doctrine of Spirit.[36] Here again we must note the close relation Tillich draws between mysticism, Greek and German idealistic ontology, and himself, over against the more biblicistic, personalistic, and judgmental viewpoint at the heart of orthodoxy and supranaturalism.

Tillich again refers to this conflict between naturalism and supranaturalism, or between the mystical or ontological and the prophetic or moral, in dealing with the fundamental tension in philosophy and theology at the end of the Enlightenment. He calls it the problem of finding "the synthesis of Spinoza and Kant."

> The relation between Spinoza and Kant became the philosophical and theological problem. Why should this be so difficult? Well, on the one side is Spinoza's mystical pantheism, as it has sometimes been called. This is the idea that there is one eternal substance, and that everything that exists is but a mode of this substance. . . . This one substance is present in everything. Here we have what I would call the principle of identity. . . . Now against this mystical pantheistic system stands Kant's philosophy, which emphasizes the principle of distance, the principle of finitude which man must accept, the transcendence of the divine beyond man's grasp and lying outside his center. . . . So all of Kant's followers and the whole continental philosophy faced this problem: How to unite the principle of identity, the participation of the divine in each of us, and the principle of detachment, of moral obedience, with-

---

between the "naturalistic" and "supranaturalist" ideas of God, cf. especially S.T., II, pp. 5-10.

[34]Nineteenth and Twentieth Century Protestant Thought, p. 20.

[35]Ibid., p. 21.

[36]Ibid., p. 20. How can a thinker reconcile a dispute with an opponent without changing the character of his own theology, so that there is no real dispute or difference left? We shall shortly have occasion to deal with this problem in terms of the distinction between the specific (situational) emphasis of a theology and its general principle.

out participation in the divine.[37]

Tillich goes on to observe that his own doctoral disserta-
tion, Mystik und Schuldbewusstsein in Schellings philosophischer
Entwicklung, dealt with Schelling's attempt to overcome this
split and that Hegel, the romantic philosophers, and above all
Schleiermacher, attempted such a synthesis, all in the spirit of
mysticism. Karl Barth, on the other hand, protests against such
mystical attempts at synthesis; he is against any form of the
principle of identity.[38]

Before we go further, we must attempt to deal with an
extremely odd thing that arises here. Let us reflect on these
last paragraphs. Tillich is saying that there is a tension
between the mysticism of Spinoza and the critical, "Protestant"
spirit of Kant. The former emphasizes identity, the latter
emphasizes contrast or judgment. But on what side are those who
attempt to unite the mystical and the moral? Are they a higher
third, or do they too lean toward one side? Tillich's seeming
answer is that their very attempt to synthesize, even when it
means uniting with their own opposite, is itself mystical,
though perhaps in a higher form. The mystical originally tends
toward complete unity through abstraction from the ambiguities
of this world, but it eventually sees that this world and its
estrangement must also be unified. And Barth's protest is not
only against the mysticism of Spinoza, but also against the more
dynamic, dialectical mysticism of Schleiermacher, Schelling, and
Hegel (and, of course, Tillich himself).

Here it is apparent how Tillich tries to be on both sides
at once.[39] The truly mystical theologian sees that he must
include or unify everything, including that which opposes such
inclusiveness. It would be as if Hegel had included Kierkegaard's
protest against him in his own system (thereby, of course,
admitting it to be a highly questionable and possibly dangerous
system). Such a mysticism would thus have a built-in protest
against itself; it is for this reason that Tillich can accept
much of Barth. What he cannot accept of those, like Barth, who
in the spirit of Kant and Protestantism absolutely reject mysticism and attempts at synthesis, is the fact that they do not
apply their protest against themselves; if they did do this,

---

[37]Ibid., pp. 74-75.

[38]Ibid., p. 75.

[39]Ibid., p. 180.

they would come near to their opposite, for they would have to
protest (however faintly one might have to do this in order to
keep from being swallowed by the abyss where all distinctions
disappear) against their own protest against mysticism.

Enough of such dizzying Tillichian dialectics: we shall
again approach this dark and necessarily bottomless issue in the
last chapter. Throughout the rest of these lectures Tillich
often returns to the view that idealistic or naturalistic ontology goes hand in hand with mysticism and that consequently the
rejection of the one is a rejection of the other. Thus "Ritschl-
ianism was a withdrawal from the ontological to the moral."[40]
In the thought of Harnack, one of Ritschl's main followers, there
is the Kantian opposition to classical ontology and mysticism in
the name of morality and this world. Harnack, Tillich says,
clearly showed the Hellenization of Christianity but did not see
the necessity of this process. Hellenization was necessary
partly because "in order to be received the Christian message
had to be proclaimed in categories which could be understood by
the people who were to receive it"; [41] that is, it was apologetically necessary.[42] But it was also necessary in order to protect the substance of the Christian message: if only the language and piety of the Old Testament were kept, as Harnack basically desired, then the whole history of doctrine as well as a
good part of the New Testament must be rejected.

> If this were to be done consistently, at least
> two thirds of the New Testament would have to
> be ruled out, for both Paul and John used a lot
> of Hellenistic concepts. Besides, it would rule
> out the whole history of doctrine. This idea is
> a new bondage to a particular development, the
> Old Testament development. Christianity is not
> nearer to the Jews than to the Greeks.[43]

We should note the relation between what emerges here and
the problem of the presence, in Tillich's theology, of arguments
from Scripture and tradition. Tillich often appeals to Scripture and tradition in his theology, but it is hard to see how
the use of such criteria could avoid an authoritarianism which
is, in principle, foreign to his theology. Tillich sometimes

---

[40] Ibid., p. 218.

[41] Ibid., p. 221.

[42] "The pagans were not Jews, and so the Jewish concepts
could not be used." (Ibid., p. 221). Thus Tillich justifies
the use of Greek concepts like ousia, hypostasis, and logos.

[43] Ibid., p. 222.

tries to claim that Scripture and tradition should not function
as criteria or norms but as <u>sources</u> of theology.[44] It is most
difficult to see just what is involved in the distinction between
a criterion and a source, especially when Tillich quite plainly
uses arguments from Scripture and tradition. Thus he attacks
the view that God is a person by appealing to the doctrine of the
Trinity,[45] to the Johannine writings,[46] to the Reformation writers,[47] and even to the words of Jesus.[48] He argues that one
reason that it is proper to call God Being-itself is because
classical theologians did.[49] He supports his emphasis on the
element of ecstasy in revelation by appealing to the prophets
and the apostles,[50] and especially to the New Testament writings
in general.[51] But on the basis of Tillich's comments about Harnack, we can perhaps see how he is using such arguments: he
believes that the Bible and tradition include various elements
which are in tension with one another, and that the tendency is
to overlook one set of these elements in favor of another. That
is, Tillich's arguments from Scripture and tradition are essentially related to the idealistic or mystical urge to include
everything, to leave nothing out; Harnack was wrong because he
left out a whole strain of the Christian experience of God, the
mystical strain. Scripture and tradition must not be used to
reject views which are <u>also</u> found in Scripture and tradition;
rather, they must be used to <u>include</u> the various elements. Only
reason can function as a negative criterion: what is blatantly
absurd or irrational, even in Scripture and tradition, must be
rejected. But what must be accepted, in defining the Christian
message, is determined by Scripture and tradition; in this sense
they are the main <u>sources</u> of Christian theology.[52] However much

---

[44]<u>S.T.</u>, I, pp. 34-40.

[45]<u>S.T.</u>, I, p. 245; <u>A History of Christian Thought</u>, p. 190;
Rome, p. 383.

[46]Rome, p. 383.

[47]<u>Ibid.</u>, p. 381.

[48]<u>S.T.</u>, II, p. 12.

[49]<u>Ibid.</u>, p. 10.

[50]<u>S.T.</u>, I, p. 111.

[51]<u>S.T.</u>, III, pp. 118, 151.

[52]Cf. <u>The Protestant Era</u>, pp. 139-140, where Tillich speaks
of "scripture or reason, the positive source and the negative
criterion of theology."

the mystical and the prophetic tend to conflict, the presence of
both sides in Scripture and tradition necessitates trying to find
some way of bringing them into some kind of unity. Thus one argument against a theological view is that it leaves something out;
i.e., that it leaves out some element in traditional Christian
experience which in part defines the very meaning of "Christian."

At the same time, it cannot be denied that Tillich himself
emphasizes certain elements in the Christian tradition over others.
Surely no one would deny that his theology somehow leans more
toward the ontological, mystical, pantheistic side than toward
the moral, prophetic, theistic (personalistic) side. Tillich
himself sometimes tried to offset this; indeed, in one of his
essays in Theology of Culture he strongly favors the prophetic or
Biblical over the mystical or Greek type of faith.[53] I believe
that here we must understand Tillich's theology on two levels;
just as, above, we saw Tillich noting the opposition between himself and Barth and yet stating that there was a way to overcome
this opposition, we must see him generally trying to do two things.
The first is to emphasize that side of faith (the mystical and
ontological) which is in danger of being overlooked today, especially because of the strange but powerful alliance between the
liberals and the neo-orthodox, while the second is to show that in
principle, i.e., apart from the existential situation of today, the
two emphases belong together. This means that we must see the
special ontological-mystical emphasis in Tillich's theology as
relative to the present situation and therefore as something which
may have to be corrected in the light of changing circumstances.[54]
This is to say only, for example, that if Tillich had lived in an
age which was too dominated by the mystical, he would (or should)
have given much less, or at least much more cautious, attention
to the value of this side of faith and correspondingly more attention to its dangers.

It is all a matter of balance. The theologian must not only
state the necessity for balance, but he himself must act to
correct the balance by, perhaps, overemphasizing elements which
have been neglected. With respect to its specific emphasis,
Tillich sees his theology as quite perishable, while with respect
to its basic principle, he sees it as eternal but also essentially

---

[53]Theology of Culture, pp. 30-39.

[54]Cf. S.T., I, pp. 47-49, where Tillich says that his fundamental norm or criterion, the New Being, is especially suited for
today, while in former generations norms like justification by
faith or the kingdom of God were best.

identical with previous theologies.[55]

It appears, then, that the particular kind of ontology or ontological language which Tillich uses is an expression of the mystical or ontological side of faith. The implication would seem to be that ontological terms such as being-itself are not mere intellectual abstractions reached by ontological or philosophical analysis (whatever that might mean[56]), but that they are expressions of a rather definite experience. Ontology would seem to be abstract not in the way that intellectualism is but in the way that abstract mysticism is: it is the expression of a very definite experience which yet cannot be described as an experience of something definite.[57] This rather odd view of ontology is substantiated by many of Tillich's remarks. He speaks, for example, of the "experience" of the New Being.[58] He says that Christianity must use philosophical terms like essence, existence, and being because "the experience and the vision behind them precede philosophy."[59] He severely chastises "the nominalists and their positivistic descendants" who think that the concept of being is the highest and thus emptiest possible abstraction, the genus of all genera, the universal of universals:

> The answer to this argument is that the con-
> cept of being does not have the character
> that nominalism attributed to it. It is not
> the highest abstraction, although it demands
> the ability of radical abstraction. _It is_
> _the expression of the experience of being_
> _over against nonbeing._ Therefore, it can be
> described as the power of being which resists
> nonbeing. . . . The same word, the emptiest
> of all concepts when taken as an abstraction,
> becomes the most meaningful of all concepts
> when it is understood as the power of being
> in everything that has being.[60] (italics mine)

Here Tillich obviously refers to the ecstatic experience of ontological shock and the overcoming of this shock.[61] He makes a similar point in discussing the highly ontological terms "idea," "essence," and "universal" in _A History of Christian_

---

[55]_S.T._, I, p. 49.

[56]See below, chapter V.

[57]For the term "abstract mysticism," cf. _A History of Chris-_
tian Thought, p. 174.

[58]_S.T._, II, p. 125.

[59]_S.T._, I, p. 204.

[60]_S.T._, II, p. 11.

[61]_S.T._, I, p. 113.

Thought. These terms, he says, arise out of the experience of astonishment; they are not mere logical abstractions.[62] They are powers of being,[63] so that "in this big tree you can see 'treehood,' and not just a big tree,"[64] They are "structures which actualize themselves again and again."[65]

If the use of the ontological concepts deriving from the Greek philosophical and mystical tradition is basically the attempt to describe an element in the experience of the holy, it becomes much easier to see just what protective value ontology has. It is true that in a sense it protects against misunderstanding the Christian message as expressed in Scripture and tradition. But when we ask what non-apologetic reason there might be for protecting against such misunderstanding, we see that again it is a matter of avoiding dangerous consequences. Those men within the church who accept a Christianity devoid of mysticism are not endangered merely because they believe the wrong thing but because their faith will tend to become profanized (powerless), as in liberalism, or else demonized, as in orthodoxy. The liberals will tend to identify religion with a set of ethical commands, while the orthodox will tend to supplant personal experience with an authoritarian demand to believe that certain strange or unintelligible assertions are true. Either way, man will be under the situation of the law, of being told to do or to believe what he lacks the power to do or believe. Thus he will either live without power altogether or else be forced to create his own power by external or internal authorities which split his communal and personal being.

Of course, it goes without saying that overlooking the prophetic element in Scripture and tradition has its own dangers. The lack of concern for the concrete will have the apologetic danger of turning away those who, for example, are interested in social reform, just as those who accept such an exclusively ontological faith will neglect man's freedom and responsibility toward other men.[66]

If this interpretation of Tillich is correct, then many questions about his reasons for using his particular type of

---

[62]A History of Christian Thought, p. 143.

[63]Ibid. p. 142; cf. also pp. 30, 79.

[64]Ibid., p. 143.

[65]Ibid.

[66]S.T., I, p. 140.

ontological language can perhaps be answered. One finds oneself asking such questions when reading, for example, his book <u>Biblical Religion and the Search for Ultimate Reality</u>. Here Tillich is purportedly dealing with precisely our problem, and yet it is, on the face of it, quite difficult to see how or whether he solves it. He nicely formulates the basic issue as that of reconciling Biblical religion and ontology,[67] and in particular the personalism of the Bible with the impersonalism of ontology.[68] Although Tillich sets out by defining ontology in a very broad way (so that it includes nominalism and personalism)[69] it soon becomes apparent that he is in fact using the term to refer to a highly idealistic or naturalistic ontology. Over half the book is devoted to showing the depth of the conflict. Ontology thinks of God as Being-itself, in which we immediately participate.[70] The Bible, on the other hand, speaks of God as a person outside ourselves addressing us through the mediation of the word.[71] "Ontology generalizes, while biblical religion individualizes."[72] Biblical religion emphasizes ethics, while ontology seems to disregard or transcend good and evil.[73]

> Is not the religious background of ontology mystical participation, whereas biblical religion presupposes the distance of ethical command and ethical obedience. . . . Is not Kierkegaard right when he accuses Hegel of sacrificing the ethically deciding person to the aesthetic distance of theoretical intuition?[74]

And so it goes for most of Tillich's book, until he slowly begins to turn the tables and show that each side presupposes elements of its opposite.[75] Biblical religion, for example, is not wholly on the side of freedom and responsibility; there are

---

[67]<u>Biblical Religion and the Search for Ultimate Reality</u>, pp. vii, 1.

[68]<u>Ibid</u>., pp. 22ff.

[69]<u>Ibid</u>., pp. 17-18.

[70]<u>Ibid</u>., pp. 27, 33.

[71]<u>Ibid</u>., pp. 22ff, 31ff.

[72]<u>Ibid</u>., p. 39.

[73]<u>Ibid</u>., pp. 43-46.

[74]<u>Ibid</u>., pp. 46-47.

[75]The reversal begins on p. 58.

also strong elements of destiny and grace in Scripture.[76] But
at this point our major question arises. What Tillich is doing
is plain enough: he wishes to reconcile the two by showing that
they differ not in principle but in emphasis. In his own words,
he is trying to show that "the attitude and concepts of biblical
religion have implications which not only allow but demand a
synthesis with the search for ultimate reality,"[77] and vice versa.
Our question is not what he is doing but why he is doing it. If,
say, biblical religion already has elements of ontology, why
make this explicit? Why not leave it implicit?

One answer, of course, is apologetic:

> It is understandable that some reject biblical
> religion completely because they are called in
> the depth of their being, in their intellectual
> and moral conscience, to ask the radical ques-
> tion--the question of being and nonbeing. They
> become heretics or pagans rather than belong to
> a religion which prohibits the ontological ques-
> tion.[78]

But how does the church itself profit from ontology? What
danger is there in not drawing out the hidden ontology of biblical religion? Why, except for apologetic purposes, show "the
structural identity of the two."[79] So far as I can see, Tillich
gives no clear answer to this question. He speaks as if all
his previous attempts to show that Bible and ontology are different are simply wrong-headed:

> The union of participation does not fall upon
> the ontological side and the distance of obedi-
> ence on the ethical side. Both sides are onto-
> logical and ethical, and both are united and
> transcended in the concept of love.[80]

But surely Tillich cannot deny his whole previous analysis.
Surely he does not mean to suggest that the whole dispute between
Hegel and Kierkegaard and between himself and Barth can be so
smoothly overcome. For if the two sides are the same, what harm
comes to a Christian who overlooks the ontological? Why are
Barth and Ritschl dangerous? Why does Tillich bother to fight
them?

The obvious answer is that Tillich tends to overstate him-

---

[76] Ibid., pp. 67ff.

[77] Ibid., p. 57.

[78] Ibid., pp. 56-57.

[79] Ibid., p. 63.

[80] Ibid., p. 69.

self in affirming that the two sides are identical. They are in
polar tension: the one side emphasizes what the other does not.[81]
If ontology is seen as the expression of the mystical side of
faith, a side of faith which is underemphasized in the Old Testament, then the New Testament, in generally using the language
of the Old, may not be able to adequately express the mystical
elements within itself. The legalistic and personalistic language of the Old Testament's moral type of faith may be unable
to express properly the mystical elements in Christianity, and
Greek philosophical language, which arose partly as an expression
of Greek mysticism, may do it better. It is for this reason
that the early church, and even some New Testament writers,
gladly used Greek concepts. Only on this basis can we understand Tillich's final words, according to which there is a tension between biblical religion and ontology, but one which biblical religion itself demands that we affirm:

> Biblical religion is the negation and the
> affirmation of ontology. To live serenely
> and courageously in these tensions and to
> discover finally their ultimate unity in the
> depths of our own souls and in the depths of
> the divine life is the task and divinity of
> human thought.[82]

Only by seeing that by "ontology" Tillich here means mysticism,
or the ontological type or side of faith, can we understand him.
Biblical religion negates and affirms ontology in the way that
the prophetic side of faith negates and affirms mysticism. Each
side needs its opposite in order to avoid destructive consequences.

Thus we have so far been able to find both an apologetic
and a protective function of ontological language in Christian
theology. The one thing we have not yet done, however, is to
discover just what ontology in general is. We have dealt only
with the question of Tillich's use of certain odd and unfamiliar
kinds of ontological language. But ontology is not, according
to Tillich, merely a special kind of language; it is also an
activity, and a logical one at that. What Tillich calls "ontological analysis" is an issue we have not yet broached. Correspondingly, we have still not done justice to the suspicion that
ontology, for Tillich, is more than a merely apologetic and pro-

---

[81] Ibid., pp. 84-85; cf. also A History of Christian Thought,
p. 30, where Tillich says of the transpersonal and personal
ideas of God: "Christianity must oscillate between these two
elements, because both are in God himself."

[82] Biblical Religion and the Search for Ultimate Reality,
p. 85.

tective device; i.e., we have not yet considered the question
of the sense in which ontological analysis may help settle questions of <u>truth</u>.

But before we deal with this matter, it is necessary first
to deal with another: Tillich's concept of a system and his
urge toward consistency. Once we have done this, we will be as
ready as we will ever manage to be to see whether some answer,
however dark, can be given to the ultimate question.

CHAPTER IV

SYSTEM, CONSISTENCY, AND COMPLETENESS

A. System and Consistency.

Why does Tillich choose the systematic form? We have seen
above that he views this form as an especially adequate way of
dealing with theological dogmas or doctrines. Dogma is "a development beyond the more primitive use of thought," for it is more
logical and methodological, but "ideally such a development
leads to a theological system."[1] But what is good about a system? The system, Tillich answers, "is necessary because it is
the form of consistency."[2] "If we understand the system. . . .
as an attempt to bring theological concepts to a consistent form
of expression in which there are no contradictions, then we cannot avoid it."[3]

This idea that consistency is the aim and justification of
the system is repeated nearly every time Tillich speaks of the
concept of a system. The fact that he makes such frequent defense of the need for thinking systematically or consistently in
theology indicates that he was quite aware that the systematic
nature of his thought was often criticized and that the criticism had to be countered again and again. Having stated clearly
in Volume I of the Systematic Theology why systematic thinking
is legitimate and necessary,[4] he returns again to his defense
in the Introduction to Volume III. He acknowledges much criticism of himself on the point: "The question 'Why a system?' has
been asked ever since the first volume of my systematics
appeared. In one of the books that deals critically with my
theology, The System and the Gospel, by Kenneth Hamilton, the
fact of the system itself, more than anything stated within the

---

[1] A History of Christian Thought, p. xii; cf. also p. 159.

[2] Ibid., p. xii.

[3] Ibid., p. xii.

[4] S.T., I, pp. 58-59; cf. also S.T., I, pp. 56-57; II, pp.
90-91; Rome, pp. 408-9 on the need for consistency; and S.T.,
I, pp. 73-74, on the function of "technical reason" in theology
"for establishing a consistent, logical, and correctly derived
organism of thought."

system, is characterized as the decisive error for my theology."[5]
Tillich notes that the same argument could be used against all
the other systems that have appeared in the history of Christian
thought, but his main argument in self-defense is the need for
consistency; in each new statement one makes one must survey
"previous statements in order to see whether or not they are
mutually compatible."[6] In his response to critics in the Kegley
and Bretall volume on his thought, he notes that "one theological
critic (Roberts) expresses a feeling, voiced by many theologians,
that there is a conflict between the existential and the systema-
tical character of every theology, including my own, and that the
systematic form threatens to choke the living quality of my
thinking."[7] But again he points out that the creation of a system involves simply the attempt to think consistently.

Thus the system is necessary for consistency. But why is
consistency necessary? Some of Tillich's answers are, so to
speak, negative: they aim to refute particular objections to
thinking consistently. One common objection is simply based on
a misunderstanding, a confusion of a system which merely seeks
consistency with a deductive system (such as Spinoza's), which
seeks far more than is legitimate in theology: namely, to derive
theological statements from non-revelatory sources.[8] "A system
is a totality made up of consistent, but not of deduced, assertions."[9] Further, the objection to consistency as such is often
rejected by Tillich on the grounds that his critics are decei-
ving themselves, for they themselves are quick to criticize the
thought of Tillich and others if they find inconsistencies.[10]
Tillich also refutes the belief that the attempt to be consistent stifles creativity and becomes like a prison: "History
shows that this is not the case"; systems have stimulated creativity as much as they have hindered it.[11]

Each of these arguments could be analyzed, but they do lit-

---

[5]S.T., III, p. 3.

[6]Ibid., p. 3.

[7]Kegley and Bretall, pp. 329-330.

[8]S.T., III, p. 3; I, pp. 58-59.

[9]S.T., I, pp. 58-59.

[10]Ibid., p. 58; Kegley and Bretall, p. 330; A History of
Christian Thought, p. xii.

[11]S.T., I, p. 59; cf. also S.T., III, p. 3.

tle to help us. To the question "Why a system?", Tillich in
effect answers "Why not?" He throws the burden of proof onto his
critics and responds by showing that in their rejection of the
attempt to think systematically, they have either misunderstood,
deceived themselves, or not looked at history closely enough. What
can we say about such a defense? What is the positive value of a
system? His first defense does not speak to our question al all;
it only shows that if one objects to a deductive system, such an
objection is not necessarily relevant to the question of mere
seeking consistency. But why then seek consistency? Tillich's
next line of defense, that his listeners seek it too, merely states a fact; it
does not answer why we should seek consistency but only that we do. And
further, what would Tillich say to one who really was not bothered
by inconsistency? Finally, the third defense shows that the
attempt to be systematic or consistent does not necessarily stifle
creativity, not why we should be consistent in the first place.
And even if we see a further argument here, namely that systematic
thought stimulates new discoveries and creativity, Tillich still
does not suggest that this is necessarily the intent of systematic
thought, but only its by-product, as it were.

Must all our attempts to find the intent or justification
for wanting to be consistent in theology be doomed to failure?
Indeed, perhaps we are being too demanding of Tillich. How
could one possibly object to the desire to make oneself consistent in any field? Is it not obviously necessary for a thinker
to be as consistent as possible? Would not everybody agree that
no one should be taken seriously who speaks inconsistently? I
would answer such an objection by saying that it seems rather
illegitimate to justify one's views by falling back upon what
everybody would agree upon; any college freshman taking a logic
course gets this point driven home to him time and again. It is
true that the same course will insist on the value of consistency,
but I am simply not sufficiently clear about the grounds for this
insistence to let the matter pass. If one says that of two
inconsistent statements, one must be false, I would like to
know what is wrong with such falsity. Is there something
immoral or dangerous or even sacrilegious about inconsistency?
Why should one expend the energy of pointing out to someone that
one of his statements has to be false? And further, we simply
must not forget that it is theology we are speaking about here,
so that any attempt to show the dangers of inconsistency in
everyday life, politics, science, or even philosophy would not
necessarily be relevant to our problem.

But we do ourselves a great injustice if we speak as if

the whole question is the perhaps odd one of how to justify
something that virtually everybody already believes in, rather
after the fashion of, say, those philosophers who ask how we can
justify believing in the existence of tables and chairs and people. The question about consistency that I have in mind is one
that is asked quite often, often enough so that such dictums as
"Consistency is the hobgoblin of little minds" or "Consistency
is the last refuge of the unimaginative" have become somewhat
commonplace. And the very fact that Tillich admits continual
criticism of his strong attempt to be consistent, whereas he is
seldom, if ever, passionately attacked for claiming that the
external world somehow exists, indicates that humanity is not
at all of one mind regarding the question of consistency.

Indeed, there is evidence to suggest that Tillich himself
was not of one mind concerning it. Although he rejects the idea
that consistent or systematic thinking is necessarily stifling,
he sometimes admits the danger that it will be. In his discussion in The History of Christian Thought, he makes an interesting admission: "The system has the danger of not only becoming
a prison, but also of moving within itself. It may separate
itself from reality and become something which is, so to speak,
above the reality it is supposed to describe."[12] And in Theology of Culture, he makes what is, in the context of our discussion, an extremely strange statement: "Now, fortunately, Freud,
like most great men, was not consistent."[13] And on the very
next page, he notes that in Sartre we have "a happy inconsistency."[14] What are we to make of this? Tillich is apparently
not at all one of those who thinks inconsistency is necessarily
bad; indeed, "most great men" are inconsistent! How can he
speak of inconsistency as something fortunate, something to be
"happy" about? How can he suggest that Freud's inconsistency,
instead of showing his stupidity, shows his greatness? Tillich
even suggests that Freud's inconsistency was a result of his
"depth" or "profundity."[15] This point may be confirmed in the
Systematic Theology, where Tillich suggests that whenever the
final revelation (or the depths of reason) is expressed in
ordinary terms, "logically contradictory statements appear. . ..
F i n a l revelation is not logical nonsense; it is a concrete

---

[12]A History of Christian Thought, p. xii.

[13]Theology of Culture, p. 120.

[14]Ibid., p. 121.

[15]Ibid., p. 121, where Tillich calls Freud "the most pro-

event which on the level of rationality must be expressed in contradictory terms."[16]

Of course, we are all aware of what is going on here: Tillich wishes to have both depth _and_ consistency. But the interest of the above passages stems from their showing that Tillich is quite willing to take seriously someone who fails to be consistent. He is not dogmatically against inconsistency, and that means that he is not one of those who take the supreme value of consistency as a self-evident truth. (He greatly respects Freud despite the fact that he was inconsistent.) And that in turn means that we might expect to find some consideration of the question why we should be consistent at all.

But Tillich's remarks on Freud and Sartre are useful for another reason: they prevent us from proceeding in what would, I believe, be an utterly fruitless direction. For sometimes Tillich gives a devastatingly direct reason for being consistent, namely, that inconsistencies are utterly meaningless. After pointing out that even the fragments of Nietzsche contain an "implicit system," he says: "So a system cannot be avoided unless you choose to make nonsensical or self-contradictory statements."[17] I believe that Tillich has overstated himself in equating unsystematic thought with nonsensical thought. The clearest example of a nonsensical-because-self-contradictory statement that comes to mind is: "There are squares that are not squares," or perhaps "There are square circles." No doubt this is sheer drivel, on any obvious definition of "square" and "circle," but it is also not the kind of thing one commonly hears people say, and I think few of Tillich's critics were demanding the right to say such things when they opposed his systematic form. Perhaps they wished to know what is wrong with speaking in, to use the jargon, "mytho-poeic" form, or perhaps they are asking what is wrong with being, like Nietzsche (or Paul?), one who keeps his "system" implicit without attempting to draw everything together. In any event, Tillich's claim

---

found of all the depth psychologists," including Jung, who over-emphasizes the essentialist and optimistic side of Freud and underplays its opposite. Cf. also p. 122, where Tillich criticizes Fromm and Jung: "In all these representatives of contemporary depth psychology we miss the depth of Freud. We miss the feeling for the irrational element that we have in Freud and in much of the existentialist literature."

[16]_S.T._, I, pp. 150-51.

[17]_A History of Christian Thought_, p. xii.

that great men, like Freud, are usually inconsistent would be
absurd if this were to mean that great men usually speak nonsense, and so would the claim that contradictions express the
depth of reason if it meant that nonsense expresses the depth of
reason.[18] Thus we must search further if we wish to find an
intelligible reason for being systematic or consistent. Unfortunately, however, Tillich seldom if ever speaks directly to the
issue, so some effort, but (I hope) not too much speculation,
will be necessary to extract some plausible answers.

B. Consistency and Apologetics.

We have come to expect an apologetic or "situational" answer,
among others, to questions about the place of intellect in theology and yet I cannot find Tillich stating unequivocally that one
reason for "explicit" consistency is that the lack of it turns
away the intellectuals; that is, his already noted attacks upon
absurdity for apologetic reasons are not clearly paralleled by
attacks upon inconsistency for apologetic reasons. Of course, it
seems rather obvious that blatant inconsistency would be so
repulsive that only the most forgiving or most vacuous readers
would remain. But it would be hard for Tillich to strongly urge
the general apologetic need for systematic consistency, for what
would he say about the high regard in the cultural world for
unsystematic thinkers like Nietzsche and, in Tillich's view,
inconsistent ones like Freud and Sartre? Absurdity, of the
literalistic type for example, obviously turns many people away
from Christianity, but what would be wrong with writing like
Nietzsche? Or like theologians such as Bultmann, Luther, or
indeed Paul, none of whom produced "explicit" systems?

And yet it is obvious that Tillich is not claiming that all
theologians should write systematically, but only that systematization has its value. Perhaps we could speculate, then, that
whatever apologetic worth the system might have is due to the
existence of people who have a particular need for, or who take
a particular delight in, systems as such. It cannot be denied
that such individuals exist; indeed, Tillich himself admits that
he is one of them. He begins his Systematic Theology with
the words: "For a quarter of a century I have wanted to write
a systematic theology. It always has been impossible for me to

---

[18]Unless, of course, the term "nonsense" were used quite
neutrally, with no connotations of stupidity or even remoteness
from the truth. But then our problem only changes its terminology:
instead of asking why avoid inconsistencies, we would ask why
avoid nonsense. It is obvious that the terms "nonsense" and "meaningless"
can be used persuasively, as the emotivists in ethics would say.

think theologically in any other than a systematic way. The
smallest problem, if taken seriously and radically, drove me to
all other problems and to the anticipation of a whole in which
they could find their solution."[19] That it was a peculiar
"need" of Tillich's to think systematically is especially evident from one of his earliest works, Das System der Wissenschaften,[20] a remarkable and almost unheard of attempt to relate all
the intellectual disciplines to one another. Why then should he
respond to this need? Why should he feel there is a value in
publishing such systems? An obvious answer, however incomplete,
would be that he was aware that other individuals had the same
need. This apologetic interpretation of the need for consistency
is also suggested in Tillich's critique of Chalcedon's doctrine
of the two natures of Christ. We have already considered this
above, but it might be well to focus more directly on exactly
what Tillich sees wrong with the "accumulation of powerful paradoxa" that Chalcedon expressed.[21] He says that the contradic-
toriness of Chalcedon has been pointed out by many;[22] it basically involves the claim that Christ was fully human and yet
fully God, i.e., not human. Why object to this? Tillich's
answer, as we have seen above but must remind ourselves, is that
it failed in its purpose of making "intelligible" to the Hellenistic mind the Christian message. The Greek "intellectuals"
required an interpretation of the message in their own terms;
this meant that the message had to be expressed with Greek philosophical concepts, but it also meant that the message had to be
expressed consistently, for this was one of the requisites of
Greek philosophical thought. But Chalcedon failed at this latter task, and thus from an apologetic standpoint did not succeed.

Although this rather hypothetical interpretation of the
value of systematic consistency is difficult to substantiate on
the basis of other and clearer statements by Tillich, perhaps it
receives some plausibility from the fact that it makes partial

---

[19]S.T., I, p. vii. Cf. also Rome, p. 408, where Tillich
says of systematic thinking: "I cannot deny that this is my
natural inclination."

[20]Das System der Wissenschaften nach Gegenständen und Methoden: Ein Entwurf (Göttingen: Vandenhoeck und Ruprecht, 1923).

[21]S.T., II, p. 141.

[22]Ibid., p. 146: "It was the merit of theological liberalism that it showed . . . the inescapable contradictions into
which all attempts to solve the Christology problem in terms of
the two-nature theory were driven."

sense of some of the rather obscure justifications for the system that we have seen Tillich give above. His justification of
the system on the grounds that even his critics demand consistency might be interpreted to mean that, so to speak, many people respond unfavorably to non-systematic or inconsistent thought
whether they are aware of it or not. His references to the presence of many systems in the Christian tradition might be seen as
a reminder that there are people who not only enjoy writing systems but also enjoy reading them: obviously writers like Calvin
and Hegel have been widely read, and part of the reason may be
their attempts to be consistent and systematic. Tillich's claim
that even fragmentists like Nietzsche have an implicit system
might be taken to suggest that in all thinkers there is an implicit (unconscious?) drive for consistency.[23] And finally, his
avowal that the system is justified because it allows us to conceive the object of theology in its wholeness and his reference
to the Gestalt character of systematics might be taken as suggestions that this is something in which not only he himself but
many others take pleasure.

Indeed, if the above interpretations are plausible, we
could even see why Tillich did not spell them out as we have
done: he did not have to. It would be, we might say, a self-
evident truth to many people (the intellectuals in particular)
that it is a desirable or, better, desired thing to see theology
in its wholeness. For then it would be enough to justify the
system on the grounds of its Gestalt character, without then
having to explain the value of seeing things as a whole. One
need not explain to children the value of cake; one need only
point out, at most, the fact that the thing over there is a cake,
and matters will take care of themselves.

The apologetic hypothesis would also explain why so many of
Tillich's justifications for the system are "negative": they
merely show that there is nothing wrong with a system. Such,
for example, is his repeated appeal to distinguish his system
from a deductive one. It is as if Tillich were saying: People
do have a need or desire for systems, thus it is legitimate to
present the contents of the Christian faith in a systematic
form, so long as we can show that we avoid the possible ethical
and religious dangers of some systems and that there is nothing
evil about the systematic form as such. If we can get more people to listen to the Christian message by presenting it system-

---

[23]See the next section for further consideration of the
concept of an "implicit" system.

atically or consistently, then by all means let us do so. Let
those who object to consistency or systematization be spoken to
by somebody else; "none of us is asked to speak to everybody in
all places and in all periods."[24]

Thus we can see Tillich as assuming an apologetic need for consistency, just as we saw him indicating the apologetic need for
nonabsurdity. Absurdity and inconsistency are two ways of being
irrational, and irrationality offends certain intellectuals.
In showing that the Christian message is not "really" absurd or
inconsistent, Tillich is showing that it is possible to formulate the Christian message in a non-absurd and consistent way,
and that such a formulation (or "translation") may be necessary
when attempting to speak to certain rational men--in particular,
to those men who define rationality partly in terms of nonabsurdity and consistency.

But however much these apologetic considerations may justify Tillich's high regard for systematic consistency, it is obvious that there is more to the matter than this. Tillich often
states that the systematic form is somehow necessary, and the
implication is that it is necessary for more than apologetic
reasons. Let us now try to see what some of these other reasons
might be.

C. Consistency and Protection.

1. Consistency and self-integration. Are there any protective reasons for avoiding inconsistency? We are immediately led
to suspect an analogy, again, between Tillich's view of the dangers of absurdity and the dangers of inconsistency. We have
seen that absurdity becomes dangerous when a person is forced to
suppress something within him, namely, his own reason. This
leads to a kind of disintegration: the person becomes split
within himself. He is told that he must not ask questions, and
yet the questions are there whether he likes it or not, and thus
he must repress them. We have seen that the questions with
which the person might be faced may have to do, for example,
with the problem of reconciling what science says with what religion says. How much more of a split-mindedness might we expect
in those who feel that they must be consistent and yet cannot
render the statements of their faith in consistent fashion?

It is plain from Tillich's writings that he felt that there
was a practical and personal danger in being told to accept in-

---

[24]Theology of Culture, p. 204.

consistencies. To expect a person to accept a contradiction
when he sees it as a contradiction (rather than as an expression
of the depths of reason) is to expect him to do something which
he cannot do without destructive consequences:

> If they [the paradoxical assertions of final
> revelation] are expressed in ordinary terms,
> logically contradictory statements appear.
> But these contradictions are not the paradox,
> and no one is asked to "swallow" them as con-
> tradictions.[25] This is not only impossible but
> destructive.

And Tillich makes clear just how this is destructive: it
splits the unity of the person by making him repress his reason.
In speaking of the attempt of the Reformers to reconcile God's
causality with man's freedom, he notes that there is no real
contradiction because the two ideas are on different levels:

> Do not think of the Reformers, or any of the
> other great theologians, in terms of a single
> level of thought. Otherwise you are faced
> with all sorts of impossible statements which
> not only contradict each other, but also result
> in the destruction of your minds, if by a heroic[26]
> effort you try to accept a contradiction.
> (italics mine)

It would be possible to show in more detail the ways or
possible ways in which Tillich sees the disintegrating effects
of inconsistency. But a great deal of what we would have to say
would closely parallel, in a rather tiresome way, Tillich's
views on the dangers of absurdity. Besides, it can be doubted
that people are quite as willing to accept blatant inconsistencies as they are to accept statements which are, by Tillich's
definition, absurd.

But one seriously wonders whether this is all there is to
our problem. Are those who reject Tillich's systematic form
really in danger of destroying their minds? And even granted
that some people may try to believe that two inconsistent statements must both be believed as factual information about God, it
can at least be asked whether this is all there is to the fuss
about theological consistency. Surely, as we have already said,
not all those who criticized Tillich's efforts to be systematic
did so because they wished to make blantantly contradictory
statements about God. Thus we might expect to find some further
sense in which inconsistency can be dangerous in theology.

    2. Consistency and completeness. But before we go further,

---

[25] S.T., I, p. 150.

[26] A History of Christian Thought, p. 269.

let us see whether we can define our problem a bit more clearly.
Tillich rarely refers to the concept of a system in the course
of his actual theological work. That is to say, he does not
explicitly argue that a given theological doctrine is invalid
simply because it is objectionable from a systematic standpoint.
But when he does his comments are puzzling, given his identification of the systematic form with consistency. In his discussion of prayer in the Systematic Theology, Tillich examines the
Ritschlian view that prayer must be limited to prayers of thanks,
thereby omitting, for example, prayers of supplication. Tillich
disagrees.

> It is therefore false to limit prayer to the
> prayer of thanks. This suggestion of the
> Ritschlian school is rooted in a profound
> anxiety about the magic distortion of prayer
> and its superstitious consequences for popular
> piety, but this anxiety is, systematically
> speaking, unfounded, although highly justified
> in practice.[27] (italics mine)

Thus Tillich admits that there is a certain practical religious
danger in the concept of praying for something, but systematic
considerations override this.

Why is this so? On the basis of Tillich's concept of the
system as the form of consistency, it would seem that somehow
Ritschl must have been inconsistent in limiting prayer to thanks-
giving. But this is surely absurd, given the usual concept of
what it is to be inconsistent--unless, of course, Tillich could
show that Ritschl had in other places somehow stated or presupposed that prayers of supplication were not objectionable. But
Tillich does not attempt to show this. Indeed, when he goes on
to explain himself, he does not openly refer to inconsistency at
all. Rather, he proceeds as follows:

> It would create a completely unrealistic
> relation to God if prayers of supplication
> were prohibited. In that case the expres-
> sion of man's needs to God and the accusa-
> tion of God by man for not answering (as in
> the Book of Job) and all the wrestling of
> the human spirit with the divine Spirit
> would be excluded from prayer. Certainly
> these comments are not the last word in the
> life of prayer, but the "last word" would be
> shallow and profanized, as innumerable prayers
> are, were the paradox of prayer to be forgot-
> ten by the churches and their members. Paul
> expresses the paradox of prayer classically
> when he speaks about the impossibility of the
> right prayer and about the divine Spirit's
> representing those who pray before God without

---

[27]S.T., III, p. 191.

> an "objectifying" language (Romans 8:26).
> It is the Spirit which speaks to the Spirit,
> as it is the Spirit which desires and exper-
> iences the Spirit. In all these cases the
> subject-object scheme of "talking to some-
> body" is transcended. He who speaks through
> us is he who is spoken to.[28] (italics mine)

This whole passage is stated as if it were to be an attempt
to show why it is systematically objectionable to exclude prayers
of supplication. But what do the arguments Tillich uses have to
do with the need for being systematic? Let us note the basic
argument Tillich uses. Tillich argues that the rejection of
prayers of supplication would create an unrealistic relation to
God because it excludes certain ordinary and traditional kinds
of prayer. In what sense would this be "unrealistic"? What
Tillich seems to be saying is that men (and particularly Christian men) always have prayed to their God and they always will
do so, that, in other words, this is an inevitable part of man's
relation to God, and thus it would be unrealistic to claim that
they should not so pray. ("Ought" implies "can," so to speak.)
Indeed, Tillich may be suggesting that it is unrealistic in a
deeper sense: the way men in fact (i.e., really) do relate to
God defines the very nature of what God is to men; it defines
the way the term God is (and therefore should be) used. The
term "God" would thus not properly apply to a being or a power
or whatever to whom one could not pray for help. Ritschl's
attempt to omit a common kind of prayer thus amounts to a new
conception of our relation to God, and thus to a redefinition of
the concept of God itself--a redefinition which the theologian
has no right to perform. Ritschl, one might see Tillich as
suggesting, has no right to demand that the term "God" be used
(by Christians) in that way.[29]

---

[28] S.T., III, pp. 191-192.

[29] We shall return to this point in the last chapter, as
well as to the obvious question: does not Tillich himself again
and again "redefine" religious symbols and concepts, above all
the concept of God? Is not Tillich far from being, as the above
remarks may suggest, what might be called an ordinary language
theologian? Does he not think that our ordinary language about
God and our ordinary concept of God are often very distorted?
To anticipate our answer to these questions: Tillich holds
that our ordinary concept of God is distorted for the very same
reason that Ritschl's was--namely, because it is exclusive. It
excludes a vast part of the Christian Scripture and tradition.
Scripture and tradition are expressions of the way Christians
have in fact related to God; thus they define the proper (Christian) meaning of the term "God." The theologian has no right
or duty or ability to change the "original" meaning of religious
symbols or concepts; he can only interpret them on the basis of

At any rate, the point is that Tillich is apparently saying that Ritschl is unsystematic because he excludes certain elements in the traditional experience of prayer. In other words, here it seems that to be unsystematic is to be exclusive, and to be systematic is to be inclusive.[30] The view of a system as the attempt to be inclusive or comprehensive would seem to fit our usual concept of a system more nearly than the view of a system as the mere attempt to be consistent. And it also more adequately fits Tillich's distinction of a system from an essay, as well as his remarks upon the Gestalt nature of a system. But we need not quarrel with Tillich's various descriptions of the system as the form of consistency; rather, we can see our results as simply clarifying what he was trying to say when he claimed that the system gives consistency. Indeed, we might suggest that Tillich did not explicitly state that the system is the attempt to be inclusive because it was so obvious that this is at least part of the point of being systematic. That is, his remarks about the nature of a system can be seen not as an attempt to give an adequate definition of "system," but as defensive remarks, remarks made in answer to certain criticisms. Tillich is answering, for example, those who wish to know how a system of his kind is different from a deductive system or why Tillich could not be equally comprehensive without using the rather forbidding systematic form. Tillich's answer is that this might have meant treating separate problems in ways that are adequate only until one tries to unite the solutions--and then irritable inconsistencies might be found. Any student of past thinkers is aware of this danger. One need only think of the history of Plato scholarship and the horrifying effort required to try to "reconcile" his different dialogues. The systematic form is thus justified because it is the attempt to avoid exactly such problems.

Thus, the best way to express Tillich's view of a system would not be simply to say that it is comprehensive (for then it might not be consistent), nor merely to say that it is consistent (for then it

---

their use in the sources and try to reconcile those which seem to conflict with one another. Thus just as Tillich the philosopher (or ontologist) seeks in Love, Power and Justice, for example, to reconcile the different meanings of the word "justice" by seeking its "root meaning," Tillich the theologian (or theonomous philosopher) seeks, in Dynamics of Faith, to reconcile the different meanings of the word "faith."

[30]For other examples of Tillich's identification of systematic thought with inclusive thought, cf. A History of Christian Thought, pp. 175, 283.

might, like an essay, not be comprehensive), but to say that a
system is supposed to be both comprehensive _and_ consistent.

But let us now focus on this matter of the importance of
comprehensiveness or inclusiveness, omitting for the moment the
issue of consistency. What does Tillich intend to be including
in his system? From his criticism of Ritschl (as well as from
the whole nature of his system) it is obvious that, in some sense,
he wishes to include, as much as possible, the various elements
in the Christian man's experience of and relation to God,[31] or,
to put it another way, the various expressions of this experience
in Scripture and tradition. The Ritschlian school, in leaving
out important elements of this experience, was unsystematic or
exclusive. Indeed, Tillich suggests that their omission overlooks the paradoxical character of prayer, turning it into "a
profanized conversation with another being called God,"[32] an all-
wise Father who hardly needs to know what we want but only asks
for our gratitude. Again and again Tillich criticizes the
Ritschlians for their exclusive personalism and consequent rejection of mysticism and Greek ontology.[33] This one-sidedness, he
claims, leads to shallowness and profanization. But have we not
heard all this before? Indeed, was not our whole last chapter
devoted to showing Tillich's belief that in Christianity as represented by Scripture and tradition the various elements of
man's relation to God are united and that things go wrong (the
consequences are dangerous) when some of these elements are
overemphasized and this implicit or essential balance is upset?
In other words, is it not the case that what we called the need
for balance in the last chapter is precisely what we are here
calling the need for completeness or comprehensiveness or inclusiveness? I believe this is true. But if so, then in considering Tillich's view of the value of being systematic (in the sense
of "inclusive"), we have perhaps elaborated upon and further
substantiated what we have already said, but we have discovered
nothing really new. We can see Tillich's attempt to be systematic in this sense as simply an attempt to further carry out his
desire for balance, to be ever more inclusive, so as to avoid
the dangerous consequences of leaving something out of the funda-

---

[31]One might best say: man's _experienced_ _relation_ to God,
in the sense that man's prayers of supplication would be described as an experienced ("felt") relation to God.

[32]S.T., III, p. 192.

[33]E.g., S.T., III, pp. 241-242, 286-287.

mental Christian message.

Thus to see the system as an attempt to be comprehensive is essentially to return whence we came. Does the same hold if we focus upon the system as the attempt to be consistent as well as comprehensive? This should not necessarily be the case, for as we have already pointed out, it is obviously possible to have completeness without consistency, just as it is possible to have the opposite. What does consistency add to completeness? Is the desire to have both simply a theoretical urge in the spirit of Greek or German philosophy? Are we to say that the only thing the church can do with respect to such systematizing is, at most, to legitimize or permit it (or, of course, urge it for apologetic purposes) among those of its flock, including its theologians, who happen to have a speculative bent? Or does the church itself have some real need for consistency? Tillich surely seems to suggest the latter. "The church cannot afford . . . to have here an insight and there an insight which . . . contradict each other."[34] But what can he mean?

To bring out our question more clearly, let us remember Tillich's evaluation of Freud as being inconsistent. And let us see Tillich as saying that Freud was sufficiently comprehensive[35] but was not consistent. Now what is wrong with that? Why not leave matters there, saying only that Freud does consider all sides if you look closely enough. Why "render" him consistent? Or let us take our results from the last chapter. If it is the case that the Bible includes both the ontological and the moral expressions of faith, why not leave it at that, merely pointing this out and not trying to make the Bible consistent? Or at most, if the Bible tends to overemphasize the personalistic because of its greater use of Jewish categories than of Greek ontological ones, why not set the two kinds of language side by side, giving equal emphasis to each? Why not simply say, for example, that God is personal and yet not personal, or that faith is both given and freely chosen, or that eternity both is and is not temporal? After all, none of these statements is meant to be a description of a state of affairs, but an expression of "the depths of reason." Or why not do as the scholars compiling the Old Testament apparently did when having to deal

---

[34]_A History of Christian Thought_, p. 159.

[35]Could we say here "deep" or "profound" instead of "comprehensive"? I suspect that "comprehensiveness" is a good part of what Tillich often means by "depth"--comprehensiveness (comprehension), that is, of the most significant human insights.

with conflicting legends expressing conflicting attitudes toward God: simply admit them all; when the J and E documents tell the same story in two ways or in different terms or with two different points, accept both stories? Or why not do as some neo-orthodox theologians do, according to Tillich: simply say yes and no to nearly every assertion about God? We would better maintain the proper balance by doing so; we would surely be more comprehensive.

I believe that in order to get into this problem we must look more closely at what Tillich says. The key is his contrast between an implicit and explicit system, or implicit and explicit consistency. For Tillich seems convinced that much thought that is not explicitly consistent is yet somehow implicitly consistent or implicitly systematic. What does this mean? What does Tillich mean when he says that Nietzsche's fragments implicitly contain a system?[36] I think it means that Nietzsche's various statements, which may seem unrelated (in the sense of inconsistent with one another), could be stated in such a way that they are consistent. Thus when, for example, Nietzsche at one time attacks Socrates in the most uncompromising terms, and in another glorifies him, we need not accuse Nietzsche of anticipating his later insanity by speaking nonsense or shifting his position from one extreme to another, nor need we choose one or the other evaluation of Socrates as expressing what Nietzsche "really" meant; rather, we can state Nietzsche's ideas in such a way that they do not conflict but only express the belief that there is something both very bad and very good about Socrates' thought: i.e., it is, as Tillich would say, ambiguous.

Let us follow out these remarks on Nietzsche. Under what circumstances, or for what reasons, might Nietzsche (or one who wished to defend him) write a book which tried to show how consistent (or "implicitly systematic") he was? Here we have Nietzsche showing us, in the words of the subtitle to Twilight of the Idols, "how to philosophize with a hammer." For many people, his words are full of powerful and illuminating insights; such admirers may feel little need to have Nietzsche systematically ordered or rendered consistent, but perhaps feel that responding to such a need would detract something valuable from Nietzsche, that it might blunt the cutting edge, the sting, of his remarks. What good would it do to try to "systematize" these insights, i.e., to render them consistent with one another?

---

[36] S.T., I, p. 58: "Nietzsche's many fragments seem to be permanently contradictory. But in all of them a system is implicit."

I can think of two practical reasons why it might be helpful to render Nietzsche's sayings consistent. In the first
place, there might be people who think that Nietzsche either contradicted himself in particular places or else changed his position from one extreme to another (and perhaps back again) in the
course of his life. Such people might thus reject Nietzsche as
not to be "taken seriously," i.e., as not to be considered one
from whom to learn something of importance or something of the
truth. They might say that Nietzsche was merely expressing his
feelings in his work, destructively ambivalent love-hate feelings
at that, feelings which led eventually to his psychological
demise. Or it might be said that Nietzsche's contradictory
utterances showed the weakness of his intellect rather than the
imbalance of his mind. At any rate, the consequence would be
that Nietzsche would be regarded as inconsistent and therefore
not to be listened to.

If Nietzsche (or one of his defenders) then wished to speak
to such people, one thing he might wish to do is to show that
the various statements are not "really" inconsistent, but only
seemingly so: that, in other words, they can be reconciled, or
expressed in such a way that the inconsistencies are gone.
Granted that this reformulation of Nietzsche might, for some, be
academic and unnecessary (since they understood the underlying
consistency in Nietzsche all along, without having to have it
made explicit), and that the "consistent" reformulation of
Nietzsche, involving qualification upon qualification, might
lack much of the power of the original. And granted that some
might feel that this systematization of his thought would neu-
tralize it, so that it no longer fully expressed, for example,
how terribly enslaving and wonderfully creative Socratic thought
is, how much we lose and gain from Socrates and even how necessary it is in general to lose much in order to gain much; granted
that, in short, systematizing might have the result of making
Nietzsche's readers think that we can easily reject the bad parts
of Socrates and keep the good ones. The point would be not to
replace the original Nietzsche with the new systematization, but
to induce people to read the original in the light of the system. The purpose would be, in short, to get certain people to
take Nietzsche seriously, to help them listen to him. One could
call this an apologetic purpose.

But there might be another purpose for rendering Nietzsche
consistent, namely, to defend Nietzsche not against his detrac-
tors but against his admirers. For his admirers, when faced,

for example, with many places where Nietzsche castigates the
Germans and many other places where he praises them, might solve
the dilemma rather easily: by deleting the one side altogether.
This could be done in many ways. It could be done crassly, as by
Nietzsche's sister who apparently just edited out the portions of
Nietzsche which spoke lowly of the Germans (compare the Marcionites of
early Christendom who wished, though without the deceptiveness of
Nietzsche's sister, to "edit out" of the canon all the Old and much
of the New Testament). Or it might be done by distinguishing the
early from the late (i.e., nearly insane or senile) Nietzsche, or
the late from the early (i.e., immature) Nietzsche (theological
comparisons here are too numerous to mention). Or it might simply be
done by saying that Nietzsche was half right and half wrong.

To counter what we believed to be misinterpretations of this
sort, we might wish to show how the apparent contradictions of
Nietzsche could be reconciled. One might wish to show, for example, that Nietzsche despised some things in the Germans and
admired others, or else that one and the same characteristic of the
Germans had both its good and bad points. One might wish to show
that Nietzsche's statements about the value of power can be reconciled with his statements about the comparative worthlessness of
mere physical or political power by showing that the kind of power
Nietzsche had in mind when praising it was the inner, creative
power exemplified better by artists like Goethe than by demagogues
like Napoleon. One's ultimate purpose in this would not necessarily
be the merely theoretical one of getting straight once and for all
what Nietzsche said; rather, it might be to keep Nietzsche from
being used by his followers for ends that would be odious to
Nietzsche himself, such as for legitimatizing Hitler, or, on the
other hand, for legitimatizing the wholesale rejection of German
culture (it would depend on what "side" of Nietzsche one accepted).
That is, the consequences of choosing one side of Nietzsche to the
exclusion of the other might be dangerous. And these consequences
might be the result of not seeing the underlying consistency in
what Nietzsche is saying. There might, in short, be a protective
aim in showing Nietzsche's consistency.

My suggestion is that Tillich is trying to make Scripture
and tradition consistent for much the same reason that an inter-
preter of Nietzsche might wish to make Nietzsche consistent.
Tillich is convinced that the fundamental insights expressed in
Scripture and tradition can be reconciled with one another
despite the fact that there often seems to be an inner contradiction between them. This is not merely to say that there is a

unity between these various elements, for then it might be the case that this unity, as soon as it is expressed in language, becomes broken. That would amount to the view that these insights cannot be comprehensively formulated in consistent terms, a view which may be that of Kierkegaard or Barth but is not that of Tillich.[37] What Tillich believes is that God is Logos (as well as power) and his revelation does not destroy man's rational structure; this means (in part) that revelation can be expressed in consistent terms. The question which then arises, as to why it should be so expressed, is given both an apologetic and a protective answer by Tillich. The theologian tries to formulate the Christian message consistently not only in order to speak to those who "need" consistency in order to listen at all, but also in order to prevent those who accept the message from dangerously emphasizing one "side" of the message to the exclusion of its opposite.

However comprehensive a thinker (or a church) is, therefore, i.e., however much he is able to balance in his writings the various insights he has been given, there will be a tendency for the balance to be dangerously upset so long as the underlying consistency between these various insights is hidden. One side, in practice, tends to be overemphasized, radically excluding the other side, no matter how much, in principle, both sides are included.

We can refer, in support of this, to Tillich's above-mentioned comments on Freud. Tillich, we have seen, says that Freud was inconsistent; his writings include two extremely important insights, the essential goodness of man and the existential estrangement of man, and yet he _formulated_ these truths in such a way that he contradicted himself: he sometimes spoke as if man were _essentially_ estranged as well as not estranged. He confused man's essential condition with his existential condition. But we wished to ask: so what? If Freud did not express himself correctly, if he did not distinguish properly between the essential and existential, what difference does it make? Somehow he was aware of both sides; i.e., he was sufficiently comprehensive or inclusive. Why also demand explicit consistency? Why not leave the consistency implicit? Tillich says of Freud:

---

[37]Of course, Kierkegaard's and Barth's suspicion of philosophical rationality and strict consistency can be interpreted in other ways, but I believe that this is how Tillich interprets it.

> In popular terms, his pessimism about the nature
> of man and his optimism about the possibilities
> of healing were never reconciled in him or in
> his followers.[38]

But what danger is there in this? Is Freud's inconsistency
merely a theoretical deficiency in Freud, or did it have practical consequences?

Tillich suggests an answer in his remarks on Freud's followers, men like Jung and Fromm. These men learned from Freud,
but they did not accept both sides of Freud. They saw the inconsistency and did the rational, or at least predictable, thing--
they excluded one of the sides:

> But some of his followers have done something
> else. They have rejected the profound insight
> of Freud about existential libido and the death
> instinct, and in so doing they have reduced and
> cut off from Freud what made him and still makes
> him the most profound of all the depth psycholo-
> gists. This can be said even in relation to
> Jung, who is much more religiously interested
> than was Freud. But Freud, theologically speaking,
> saw more about human nature than all his followers
> who, when they lost the existential element in
> Freud, went more to an essentialist and optimistic
> view of man.[39]

Jung and Fromm, Tillich says, tended to think of the human
situation as "correctible and amendable, as a weakness only."[40]
These men have overly optimistic hopes for man, and Tillich often
points out the concrete dangers of such optimism.[41] But the
point to notice here is the suggestion that the dangerous one-
sidedness of Freud's followers was a result of Freud's inconsistency. We might suppose that Tillich would hold that if Freud
had been more systematic, i.e., if he had taken more pains to
reconcile the seeming inconsistencies in his thought, the danger
that his followers would become one-sided may have been lessened.
There would have been less tendency to accept one side of Freud
and throw out the other.

Comprehensiveness, in short, seems to be something which is
extremely unstable, since the fundamental insights about man and
God are in polar tension. Consistency is a means of adding a
certain stability; it is, in Tillichian language, a means of

---

[38] Theology of Culture, p. 120.

[39] Ibid., p. 120-121.

[40] Ibid., p. 121.

[41] Cf. for example, A History of Christian Thought, p. 120;
S.T., III, p. 348.

grasping (and holding onto) these insights.[42] Without consistency, one eventually tends to lose the vital balance; what was
a dynamic tension becomes a demonic split.

We can think here of Chalcedon's doctrine of the two natures
of Christ. Tillich, we have seen, holds that Chalcedon protected
the substance of the Christian message. We can take this to mean
that it included two very important sides, either of which, if
emphasized to the exclusion of the other, has dangerous consequences. And yet it can hardly be denied that the Christian
church has seldom been able to hold the sides together: there
has always been a tendency to overemphasize either the humanity
or the divinity of Christ. Faced with an apparent contradiction,
the general tendency is to choose one side.

Thus it must, for practical purposes, be shown that the two
sides can be reconciled; it is not enough merely to claim that
they are united beneath the level of language or in the mind of
God. This is not necessarily to say that everybody will need to
be shown this. Some will be able to see the underlying consistency in Nietzsche's thought without ever explicitly formulating
it. Some will be able to see the underlying consistency in
Scripture without creating a system. But others will have to be
clear about the consistency or else they will tend to one
extreme. This means that insofar as Tillich is a systematic
theologian, he is not merely trying to state both sides but to
reconcile them.

On this basis we can find another motif in Biblical Religion
and the Search for Ultimate Reality. We have already seen, in
the last chapter, that one of the things Tillich was trying to
do in this book was to give proper emphasis to the ontological
or mystical element in faith, an emphasis which, he thinks, is
found or presupposed in Scripture itself. Thus a great deal of
the book is devoted to showing how the difference between biblical religion and ontology is a matter of emphasis. The Bible

---

[42]One might say that reason (or conceptual thought), for
Tillich, is partly the attempt to grasp (or retain) what one
has been grasped by. This grasping is necessary because revelatory moments are temporary; they pass, and thus man must attempt
to grasp in language and thought the fullness of what one has
seen. Cf. S.T., III, p. 115: "After the experience, the
teacher can analyse and formulate the element of meaning in the
ecstasy of inspiration (as the systematic theologian does), but
when the analysis of the teacher begins, the inspirational experience has already passed." Cf. also S.T., III, p. 202: "The
meditative act penetrates the substance of the religious symbols; the discursive act analyzes and describes the form in
which the substance can be grasped."

stresses freedom and the concept of a personal God; ontology
stresses determinism and the concept of an impersonal Absolute.
And yet, upon deeper analysis, we see within the Bible itself
suggestions contrary to the exclusive ideas of free decision and
a personal God, and we see within ontology suggestions contrary
to those of a sheer necessity and an impersonal, non-transcendent
God. But we saw that if this is all Tillich wishes to say, then
it would be hard to distinguish him from theologians who believe,
say, that there is an inner inconsistency in biblical thought
and that this is due to the inadequacy of language and reason to
consistently express both sides of the experience of the holy.

But Tillich wishes to go beyond this. He wishes to show, in
a rather Hegelian way, that there is an ontological or philosophical way of stating both sides in consistent fashion. There
are suggestions within his book that the conflict between biblical religion and ontology, (or between the moral and the ontological types of faith), can be reconciled by a "third way": a
higher kind of ontology in which the two sides are not only
stated together in a combined yes and no, but reconciled by
showing their consistency.

For example, Tillich says that the Bible is at odds with
itself on the question of the personalism of God, for it sometimes speaks of God in terms which transcend the personal. The
biblical writers knew that if God is merely a person, he is subject to the structures of being, to fate, as Zeus was.

> The fight against this dangerous consequence
> of biblical personalism started in the Bible
> itself and continued in all periods of church
> history. The God who is a being is transcended
> by the God who is Being itself, the ground and
> abyss of every being. And the God who is a
> person is transcended by the God who is the
> Personal Itself, the ground and abyss of every
> person.[43]

But does this mean that we must suspend our reason, our
attempt to understand how God can be both personal and beyond the
personal at once? That is, must we give up the attempt to make
these seemingly inconsistent ideas consistent? No, says Tillich:

> This means that being and person are not contra-
> dictory concepts. Being includes personal being;
> it does not deny it. The ground of being is the
> ground of personal being, not its negation.[44]
> (italics mine)

It may well be that Tillich, in such statements, does not

---

[43]Biblical Religion and the Search for Ultimate Reality,
pp. 82-83.

[44]Ibid., p. 83.

do adequate justice to the idea of a personal God. We are not
here concerned, however, with criticizing Tillich but in attempting to see his intent. And his intent is clearly to make consistent these two different experiences of the nature of God,
not just to state them together.

We must again remind ourselves just what is at stake here.
The temptation in reading Tillich is to be, in a sense, too easy
on him. He continually states that if we are to understand the
two sides, we must reconcile them by removing their inconsistencies.[45] That is, if we are to deal theoretically with religious
language, we must reconcile in thought its apparent contradictions. But we have already made clear that we do not regard
this as a sufficient answer, for it can easily be asked why we
should understand or deal theoretically with or think about religious language--i.e., in this context, why we should make it
consistent. If religious language does not give factual information but simply expresses something, why demand consistency of
it? Do we demand of poetry that it be consistent? If a poet or
religious thinker believes that he can express himself properly
only by making logically inconsistent assertions, must we rele-
gate what he says to the realm of non-cognitive feeling? Have
not the logical positivists been, if not refuted, at least intelligently questioned regarding such points, regarding, that is,
their presuppositions about the nature of reality, knowledge,
and language which are involved in such claims as well as the
value of that kind of reality, knowledge, or language which
requires proper rational formulation?

Thus it could at least be argued that explicit consistency
is a requisite in theology no more than (or even less than) in
poetry. We have previously seen that one reason Tillich rejects
such a claim is an apologetic reason and that another reason is
similar to his rejection of absurdity: that consistency protects
against a "destruction of the mind" (for those whose minds
demand consistency). Here we are dealing with a third reason,
or a second protective reason: that consistency helps prevent
a dangerous exclusiveness.

But again, we do not have to claim that Tillich succeeds in

---

[45]E.g., he says that the tension between God's action and
man's free response "can be understood only through the ontological polarity of freedom and destiny and through a distinction
between the levels of being" (Ibid., p. 80). And "the ontological question of being creates not a conflict but a necessary
basis for any theoretical dealing with the biblical concept of
the personal God" (Ibid., p. 83).

attaining this proper balance; we do not have to say that his
attempt to be consistent and comprehensive really is successful.
(Indeed, Tillich does not think that the attempt ever will be
completely successful, however possible it is in principle: he
often criticizes Hegel on this score. Hegel was right in
claiming that the truth is the whole; he was wrong in thinking
that he had the whole.)[46] Nor need we claim that we understand
the incredibly abstract formulations which result when Tillich
tries to make apparently conflicting assertions about God consistent with one another: I myself would be the last to make such
a claim. We are merely interested in Tillich's intent in trying
to be consistent as well as comprehensive. We are interested in
seeing how Tillich's highly rationalistic demands for such
things as consistency are supposed to serve the church.

We have already indicated a few places where Tillich shows
that he was interested not only in comprehensiveness but also in
consistency. To show the others would be tantamount to repeating most of his theology. For his general theological effort is
directed toward finding a way of stating two seemingly inconsistent answers to a given question in a consistent way. He is
continually trying to find a way of stating things so as to overcome or go beyond or transcend a seeming conflict. The "basic
intention" of his doctrine of God, he says, can be expressed in
the terms: beyond naturalism and supranaturalism.[47] "An idea
of God which overcomes the conflict of naturalism and supranaturalism could be called 'self-transcendent' or 'ecstatic.'"[48]
Revelation is not merely rational, nor is it merely ecstatic or
emotional; it is both at once: reason is not destroyed but
preserved and elevated, although transcended.[49] Theonomy is the
transcendent union of autonomy and heteronomy.[50] With respect
to the question of whether in speaking of Jesus as the Christ we
refer to a historical person or the subjective reception of
Jesus as the Christ, Tillich says: "We cannot speak the truth
about the event on which Christianity is based without asserting
both sides";[51] the two sides must be "emphasized with equal

---

[46]S.T., III, p. 255.

[47]S.T., II, p. 5.

[48]Ibid.

[49]S.T., I, pp. 113-114.

[50]Ibid., pp. 147-150.

[51]S.T., II, p. 98.

strength,"[52] and Tillich goes on not only to state them but to
make rational (i.e., consistent) the two. Eternal life must be
understood not as mere timelessness nor as endless time but as,
somehow, both together.[53]

To show whether Tillich offers an intelligible reconcilia-
tion of the two sides in these cases is, again, not part of our
task, but it might clarify matters if we looked more closely at
a concrete example. A simple case is Tillich's handling of the
problem of the need for moral action versus the awareness that
not in history, but only in "the eternal now" is there salvation.
Emphasizing merely the former (the moral side) leads to fanaticism and eventually to disillusionment (i.e., to demonic and then
profane consequences); emphasizing merely the latter (the ontological side) leads to a withdrawal from the demands for justice
and social action.[54] How can one preserve an interest in social
action along with a realistic understanding of the impossibility
of an everlasting utopia? Tillich answers with his concept of
kairos, according to which, quite simply, "history has its ups
and downs."[55] History is not unchanging with respect to the
extent of justice; there are high points and we can and should
work toward them. But "history shows" that we must expect down-
swings; thus we must not be disappointed by the failure of an
absolute utopia. In this way Tillich is able to claim two
things: that we should work for justice and yet realize that we
will fail, but he is also able to show how these two claims,
based respectively on the "insight" that justice is demanded and
the "insight" that man is estranged and thus cannot, in history,
expect to attain it, are not inconsistent. The concept of
kairos is an attempt to reconcile these demands.

Of course, these remarks do not do justice to the richness
of Tillich's concept of the kairos, and they do no justice at
all to his concept of the unique kairos which appeared in Jesus
as the Christ. The only point is that Tillich seems to be suggesting, or at least presupposing, that in order to act properly,

[52]Ibid.

[53]S.T., I, pp. 274-276. Cf. also the pair of double negative statements (supplemented by a metaphor to give positive
meaning) throughout the last section of Tillich's Systematic
Theology on the various problems regarding the concept of eternal life (S.T., III, pp. 394ff).

[54]A History of Christian Thought, pp. 119-120. Here Tillich
refers to the conflict in Augustine "between mystical-ontological
thinking and ethical-educational thinking."

[55]S.T., III, p. 371.

i.e., for practical purposes, we must not merely see the truth of
both sides but must see the unity of these truths. And throughout Tillich's work, the implication can hardly be avoided that to
the extent that we can express the two sides consistently, to
that extent will we be better able to avoid the concrete dangers
of overemphasizing only one.[56]

In all this we can compare Tillich to those in the ancient
church whom he calls the "jurists."

> The tradition . . . was composed of many
> elements, not all of which said the same
> thing . . . Thus, _practical_ _needs_ created
> a class of people whose task it was to _har-_
> _monize_ the different authorities on the
> meaning of the canon laws, as they appear
> in the many collections of canon law. This
> harmonizing method was a dialectical method,
> the method of "yes" and "no," as it was
> called. Reason in the Middle Ages was the
> tool for this purpose.[57] (italics mine)

Thus the attempt to reconcile or harmonize the elements in
tradition is quite a practical one. Tillich again refers to the
relation between dialectics and the practical needs of the Church
when speaking of the main trends in Scholasticism:

> The first form in which autonomous thinking
> arose in the Middle Ages was dialectics. . . .
> We have already mentioned how the jurists, who
> represented the canon law, had to harmonize for
> practical reasons the different authorities,
> councils, and theologians. Out of this need
> there arose the method of dialectics, of "yes"
> and "no."[58]

And again, in speaking of Abelard's theology, Tillich notes

---

[56]We should note that Tillich does not seem to think that a
mere _emphasis_ on one side is necessarily dangerous; indeed, his
view of the dialectical dynamics of life seems to require a variety of emphases. What is bad (demonic) is _overemphasis_. Not
action and reaction, but over-action and over-reaction are the
essence of the demonic. There is a difference between a tension
and a split. Note that in his discussion of Augustine, Tillich
admits his own emphasis upon the non-utopian, and he is quite
aware that this may be too much emphasis: "This would be my
decision, and yet it is a very questionable one" (A History of
Christian Thought, p. 120). The point is that we cannot be sure
of avoiding dangers, but we must decide anyway. In general,
Tillich holds that "dangers are not a reason for avoiding a serious demand" (S.T., III, p. 4). That Tillich comes within a
hair's breadth (at least) of making sin a necessity in statements
like this is a point I need hardly make since nearly everybody
makes it, though seldom with a sensible alternative.

[57]A History of Christian Thought, p. 138.

[58]Ibid., p. 140

that Abelard, too, used dialectical thinking for practical reasons:

> Abelard represents the type of jurisprudential
> thinking which was introduced into Western
> Christianity by Tertullian. He was, so to
> speak, the lawyer who defended the right of the
> tradition by showing that the <u>contradictions</u> in
> <u>its sources</u>--which no one can deny--<u>can be
> solved.</u>[59] (italics mine)

Here Tillich makes quite clear that the church has a practical interest in resolving its inconsistencies. And Tillich
even compares himself with Abelard.[60] In part, the practical
problem seems to have been an apologetic one: Abelard "defended
the right of the tradition" through his dialectical method. But
did a non-apologetic problem exist as well? Tillich's answer is
affirmative:

> The <u>practical</u> <u>problem</u> was that the pope and his
> advisors <u>had to make decisions</u>, and they wanted
> them to be based on the tradition of law. So
> the law had to be harmonized.[61] (italics mine)

If we substitute for "the pope and his advisers" the words
"all Christians" (applying the Protestant doctrine of the priest-
hood of all believers), we can see Tillich as suggesting that
within the church it is necessary to harmonize the different
elements in the tradition because otherwise one will have to
exclude certain valuable elements of the tradition--and such
exclusion or exclusiveness is, as we have seen, dangerous.
Christians must act or decide, and if they neither implicitly
understand nor can explicitly be shown how opposing elements in
the tradition can be reconciled, they will have to choose some
and reject others. Comprehensiveness is not enough; the pope
and his advisers had that. What they needed was one who could
make the comprehensive tradition consistent. This is how the
search for consistency can serve the church. And this is why
the delight of the systematic (or dialectical) theologian lies
in finding consistencies:

> Then it might be shown that what seemed to be
> contradictions are not such at all, but only
> different forms in which the very same idea
> is expressed. It happens often in the history
> of thought that statements contradict each
> other only when taken as isolated statements
> out of the <u>Gestalt</u>, the structure, to which

---

[59] <u>Ibid.</u>, p. 168.

[60] <u>Ibid.</u>, pp. 167-168.

[61] <u>Ibid.</u>, p. 169.

> they belong. While appearing contradictory,
> they may actually say one and the same
> thing.[62]

We could go far beyond what we have said here by entering into a discussion of the peculiarly paradoxical nature of Christianity according to Tillich. The point would be that Christianity is especially liable to fall into dangerous inconsistencies and thus overemphasis because of the very deep tension within it, a tension much deeper than any found even in Hegel's dialectical system. Decisive here would be Tillich's concepts of sin and grace, as well as his pivotal concept of the New Being in Jesus as the Christ (all paradoxes in Christianity, including the simul justus et peccator understanding of the doctrine of justification by faith through grace, are derived from this one).[63] But I doubt that this is necessary; and even if it were necessary, my ontological abilities are not equal to such a task. At any rate, the principle of the matter would remain the same; the only real difference is that eventually Tillich can avoid inconsistency only with the greatest effort and only after being reduced to using double negations in conjunction with poetic metaphors.[64]

---

[62] Ibid., p. 170. Tillich almost presupposes that any major dispute is no real dispute at all. For example, in asking why thinkers have been almost equally divided on the question of the validity of the arguments for the existence of God, he says that this dispute "admits of only one explanation: the one group did not attack what the other group defended" (S.T., I, p. 204; cf. also A History of Christian Thought, p. 165). I believe that this presupposition has to do with his doctrine of the goodness of creation: if one gets to the heart of any powerful viewpoint, one will see its truth and goodness (and also how this original truth and goodness have been distorted). Demonic ideas are not created ex nihilo, but are distortions of something originally or basically good.

[63] S.T., II, p. 92.

[64] See footnote 53, above. I believe that ultimately all Tillich's statements about the two concepts which he eventually identifies, God and Eternal Life (S.T., III, p. 421), would have to take the form of double negations plus metaphor. I.e., just as Tillich wishes to say of eternal life that it is not timelessness and that it is not endless time, he wishes to say of God that he is not any kind of essence and that he is not any kind of existence (or existing thing). I sometimes suspect that Tillich's claim that God is being-itself is really a negative statement, or rather a pair of them: it may mean that God is not a being, i.e., that he is not anything in particular, but that he is also not something in general, i.e., a universal or essence or ideal. He is the "ground" of both essence and existence (S.T., I, pp. 236-237). That is, he "precedes" the existential split between essence and existence. Here we have two negative assertions, the positive content being filled by metaphorical expressions like "ground."

Rather than continuing on the same track, therefore, I wish to see whether we are now able to make a final attempt to understand Tillich's use of ontology. In a sense, we could say that in this chapter we have found another use for ontology, namely, to assure consistency and thus to maintain balance. But this would be so like the use of ontology which we analyzed in the previous chapter that it would not be a decisively new use, but only a natural extension: it is obvious that the idealistic ontologist tries to be both comprehensive and consistent, in some sense. What we wished to find in this chapter is why the theologian is interested not only in comprehensiveness but also in consistency.

What we must now do, therefore, is to embark upon an attempt to understand what Tillich sees as the aim of ontological analysis, and in particular how such analysis helps serve the church. Here we return to the problem of ontology for the third time, and perhaps at last we will be able to get some understanding of the question whether ontology not only has an apologetic and protective role in theology, but also functions to provide religion with some otherwise inaccessible kind of truth.

CHAPTER V

ONTOLOGY ITSELF

A. Some Remaining Problems

There are two problems (at least) with which we have not yet
dealt, and both have to do with issues which cannot, it would
seem, be reduced to the realm of the practical. These problems
both seem to require a strictly theoretical orientation; they
indicate points in theological reflection at which theology seems
to be doing more than something apologetic or protective. The
first of these has to do with the aim and function of ontology or
philosophy. Can ontology, insofar as it is used in theology, be
reduced to functioning either as a means of expressing the Christian message to the intellectuals or as a means of expressing and
thus properly emphasizing (protecting) the ontological or mystical
element in faith? Have we done full justice to Tillich's use of
ontology so far? It cannot be denied that in our two former chap-
ters on ontology we have dealt with ontology in a rather superfi-
cial way. That is, we have dealt with ontology only as a kind of
language, a way of speaking. We have not tried to get within
ontology itself so as to see what the ontologist is trying to do.
But surely ontology is more than a way of speaking, at least for
Tillich. It is a kind of reflection upon or analysis of certain
problems. It does a kind of reflection upon or analysis of certain problems. It does no more justice to Tillich's concept of
ontology to call it a way of speaking than it would do justice to
the scientist's concept of science to call it a way of speaking.
This would leave out, for example, the questioning and proving
aspects of science; to speak more plainly, it would leave out the
sense in which the scientist claims to be giving some kind of theoretical knowledge about the world. Have we not similarly reduced
ontology to something which Tillich himself would reject?

But there is another problem with which we have not dealt.
Despite all our attempts to show that theology has very practical
criteria for judging itself, criteria having to do with apologetic power and the avoidance of demonic and profane consequences, there remains an undeniable theoretical resudue. We
have made theology into something very pragmatic, and yet
Tillich himself, while accepting the presence of pragmatic elements in theology, often criticizes pragmatism because it "lacks

103

á criterion."[1] He notes that one can always ask of the pragmatist whose criterion is success the question as to the criterion by which one judges whether one has been successful:

> If the successful working of the principles is called the "criterion," the question arises, "What is the criterion of success?" This question cannot be answered again in terms of success, that is, pragmatically.[2]

The point here is that somehow one must have, apparently, a principle which is not itself pragmatic but theoretical. Of course, we have seen that Tillich has such principles, in a sense, for he judges the "success" or value of a given theological or religious assertion by the demonic or profane consequences of accepting it as well as by its bare apologetic power. But surely we can ask how Tillich is so sure that the demonic and the profane (in _his_ sense) are bad, or where he gets the principles with which he judges something to be demonic or profane--i.e., how he decides whether particular consequences are demonic or profane.

We can relate this point to our diatribe, in chapter two, against the value and even the possibility of "getting straight" what Christianity is saying.[3] We showed there that Tillich believes that dogma does not protect against merely misunderstanding, intellectually, the Christian message, but against demonic and profane consequences. But can Tillich claim that all dogma is negative or protective in this sense? Surely there must be some other dogma or dogmas which are _positive_ and thus provide the means for determining what, according to Christianity, _constitutes_ the demonic and the profane and for determining that the demonic and the profane are _dangerous_.

Indeed, Tillich admits that there is one positive doctrine in Christianity: the doctrine of the New Being in Jesus as the Christ.[4] (He also calls this doctrine the material norm or criterion for his theology.[5]) This is obviously, however, an ontological principle, or at least a principle stated partly in ontological terms. Further, Tillich claims that the failure of pragmatism to provide a criterion means that we must have an ontological criterion. The highest criterion is always some

---

[1] S.T., I, pp. 104-105; S.T., III, pp. 28-29.

[2] S.T., I, p. 105.

[3] See above, 30ff.

[4] A History of Christian Thought, p. xiv; S.T., II, p. 92.

[5] S.T., I, pp. 49-50.

"ontological principle which cannot be tested pragmatically because it is the criterion of all testing."[6]

What I am saying is that there is a relation between the two theoretical problems with which we have not yet dealt. Both have to do with ontology. Somehow ontology is what provides us with the ultimate norms for decision, or, to state it another way, our ultimate norms are ontological whether we know it or not. Thus we might expect to be able to solve both problems by dealing with Tillich's view of the nature of ontology.

But before trying to understand Tillich's concept of ontology, we should point out that there is one more problem with which we have not dealt, although it is not a theoretical but the most practical problem of all. It is the question, to which we have referred several times before,[7] of the _effectiveness_ of theological argument. Is there not a point at which all argument must fail, and is it not true that in principle there is no way to argue with somebody whose basic presuppositions one does not share? This is a common enough view, but we have suggested that the situations in which this question can be asked may be much more numerous than we might think, and that this fact may even explain why theology seems to have made so little progress toward agreement or why a given theological debate, even (or especially) among renowned theologians, often leaves one with the sinking feeling that nothing was accomplished, that the truth is as far away as ever. Thus when two theologians disagree over what is or is not Christian, and if they try to settle the debate by appeals to Scripture and tradition (or any part thereof), is it not apparent that the issue can seldom be settled that way? Do not so many unshared presuppositions enter in that any hope for agreement is mere wishful thinking? "So it is," someone might say, "and that is why theologians should appeal to reason rather than to authority." But is reason in any better shape? Has the long line of philosophers been any more successful in finding and agreeing upon the truth than the theologians? Or, not to blaspheme philosophy, have those theologians who have claimed to get their conclusions from reason been any more successful in agreeing among themselves than those who admittedly depend upon authority?

There is indeed a strange paradox here. If theologians are united in their ultimate presuppositions, why do they not

---

[6] _S.T._, III, p. 29.

[7] Cf., e.g., above, pp. 31-32.

eventually come to agreement? But if, on the other hand, they
are _not_ so united, why do they not realize that fact and thus
cease arguing, since no arguments could succeed?

It is apparent that here the most theoretical and the most
practical problems merge, and they merge around the issue of
presuppositions or _ultimate_ _criteria_ or _first_ _principles_. Might
we not, then, hope to gain some insight into all of them by considering Tillich's view of ontology? Perhaps we could at least
allow ourselves to hope so, for without such a hope only the
most masochistic of motives could propel us to delve more deeply
into Tillich's abstract ontological reflections. At any rate,
let us proceed.

B.   The _Nature_ _of_ Ontology

What is ontology, according to Tillich? In attempting to
answer this question, we must try to distinguish between
Tillich's definition of ontology as such and his description of
his own particular kind of ontology; we wish to confine ourselves
to the former. In the _Systematic_ _Theology_, Tillich first deals
with the nature of ontology in discussing the relation between
theology and philosophy.[8] Here it becomes clear that he uses
the terms "philosophy" and "ontology" more or less interchangeably, or, more properly, that he offers what he calls an "ontological definition of philosophy," and he also states that what
he calls "ontology" is what has traditionally been called "meta-
physics," though the latter term now has misleading connotations.[9] Now what is it that ontology, philosophy, or meta-
physics is trying to do?

Tillich's most common answer is that it asks the question of
being:

> The ontological question is: What is being
> itself? What is that which is not a special
> being or a group of beings, not something con-
> crete or something abstract, but rather some-
> thing which is always thought implicitly, and
> sometimes explicitly, if something is said to
> be? Philosophy asks the question of being as
> being.[10]

This is not entirely clear. Tillich goes on to say that
"ontology is possible because there are concepts which are less

---

[8]_S.T._, I, pp. 18ff.

[9]_S.T._, I, pp. 20, 163; _Biblical_ _Religion_ _and_ _the_ _Search_ _for_
Ultimate _Reality_, p. 6.

[10]_S.T._, I, p. 163.

universal than being but more universal than any ontic concept,
that is, more universal than any concept designating a realm of
beings."[11] Tillich lists several levels of ontological concepts,
and then he treats of the epistemological character of ontological concepts. They are strictly a priori, but only in the sense
that they are presupposed whenever something is experienced.[12]
They constitute the structure of human experience, as it has
been known historically.[13]

What we can gather from this is at least the following:
that ontology has to do with presuppositions, presuppositions
which structure our experience or make sense of it. And these
presuppositions have to do with certain fundamental concepts.

So far as I can see, Tillich is clearest in describing the
nature of ontology in Love, Power, and Justice. He notes that
the first task in discussing these three concepts is to find
their "root meaning":

> Therefore we must ask whether there is a root
> meaning in each of these concepts, determining
> their use in the different situations to which
> they are applied. Such a basic meaning would
> precede in logical validity the variety of
> meanings which could be derived from it. There-
> fore the search for the basic meaning of love,
> power, and justice individually must be our
> first task, and it must be carried out as a part
> of the search for the basic meaning of all those
> concepts which are universally present in man's
> cognitive encounter with his world. Traditionally
> they are called principles, structural elements,
> and categories of being. Their elaboration is
> the work of ontology. Ontology is the way in
> which the root meaning of all principles and
> also of the three concepts of our subject can
> be found. . . Ontologically we shall ask for the
> root meaning of love and of power and of justice.
> And if we do so, we may discover not only their
> particular meanings but also their structural
> relation to each other and to being as such.[14]
> (italics mine)

Tillich seems to feel that many disputes hinge upon disagreement over certain fundamental words or concepts, and that if
such disagreement is to be overcome it can be done only by ascer-
taining the root meaning of these concepts. People disagree
over the nature or essence of justice, and they also disagree

---

[11] Ibid., p. 164.

[12] Ibid., p. 166.

[13] Ibid., p. 167.

[14] Love, Power, and Justice, pp. 1-2.

about the relation, for example, between justice and love (e.g., are justice and love mutually conflicting ideals or are they dependent upon one another?) Ontology can help settle such conflicts.

One can see Tillich pursuing this method throughout his works. As an ontologist strictly speaking, he deals with concepts such as community, the individual, power (dynamics), form, justice, freedom, and destiny. As an ontological theologian he seeks the root meaning of concepts and symbols such as God, faith, miracle, sin, revelation, and eternal life.

Thus ontology is not "speculative" but, as Tillich says, descriptive:

> It is never "speculative" in the (unjustified) bad sense of the word, but it is always descriptive, describing the structures which are presupposed in any encounter with reality. Ontology is descriptive, not speculative.[15]

And further, ontology can be considered to be analytical. "It analyzes the encountered reality, trying to find the structural elements which enable a being to participate in being."[16]

The term "structure" is used again and again in describing ontology, but it is not clear what this means. Indeed, in the Kegley and Bretall volume on his thought, Tillich is directly asked what the word means and he admits that it is "not definable."

> There are notions which resist definition and whose meaning can only be shown by their configuration with other notions. The basic ontological concepts fall in this category.[17]

At least we could expect Tillich to give some examples of structures. I suspect that what he means here is, at least in part, related to his concepts of "root meanings" and presuppositions. It has to do with the ideal (or "real") meaning of a term. I believe that Tillich would have willingly used the term "essences" instead of "structures" were it not for the fact that he also wishes to speak of existential structures such as estrangement, which are "structures of destruction";[18] they involve a distortion of the essential.

What, though, is Tillich getting at when he speaks of ontology as a kind of analysis? It seems that he is opposing analy-

---

[15]Ibid., p. 23.

[16]Ibid.

[17]Kegley and Bretall, p. 330.

[18]S.T., II, p. 60, Rome, pp. 399-400.

sis here to argument or proof or derivation. Ontology deals
with starting points, with what is presupposed rather than with
what is proved (either deductively or inductively). To say that
ontology is a kind of analysis is thus similar to saying that it
is descriptive. The distinction between an analysis and an
argument is made, for example, when Tillich criticizes the arguments for the existence of God.[19] These are not, he says, arguments (which prove that there is a being called God); rather,
they are "ontological analyses."[20] They point to "something
unconditional in every encounter with reality,"[21] some absolute
standard, so to speak. The awareness of an ultimate "is not the
result of an argument but its presupposition."[22]

The question, however, is how one gets at these presuppositions. How does one go about determining the "true" meaning of
faith or love or justice or God? To put the question more
pointedly, how would we go about settling a dispute over the
true meaning of these concepts? For Tillich to say that the
ultimate criteria of any judgment must be ontological can, in
view of his concept of ontology, be seen as saying that the ultimate criteria cannot be proved or derived or argued for but are
presupposed. But surely different people can have different
presuppositions. Is it not the case, then, that Tillich is
saying that each person has his own ontological criteria (his
own God or gods, if you will) by which he settles matters for
himself, but that these criteria may not be objectively (inter-
subjectively) valid? But if this is so, then is not the whole
point of ontological analysis, the search for root meanings or
presuppositions, undercut? Was not ontology supposed to get us
to some common ground? But how can it do so, if people have
different presuppositions and if these presuppositions cannot
be argued for, being the starting points for the arguments themselves?

This is indeed a strange paradox. Perhaps it would be good
to see whether Tillich offers any way of solving it. For if he

---

[19] S.T., I, pp. 204-207.

[20] Ibid., p. 207.

[21] Ibid.

[22] Ibid., p. 206. Cf. also Rome, p. 398, where Tillich
rejects his own previous use of the term "deriving" for the
relation of value to being.

does not, it is most difficult to see any more point to ontology in theology than the strictly practical (apologetic and protective) ones with which we have already dealt.

C. The Verification of Ontology

1. Recognition versus argument. Let us present our question as follows. What kind of argument would be relevant to a dispute over ontology? How, for example, would one go about trying to convince somebody that his ontology is defective? Tillich gives an answer to this question in Love, Power, and Justice, but it does not seem to take us very far.

> Is there a way of verifying ontological judgments? There is certainly not an experimental way, but there is an experiential way. It is the way of an intelligent recognition of the basic ontological structures within the encountered reality, including the process of encountering itself. The only answer, but a sufficient answer, which can be given to the question of ontological verification is the appeal to intelligent recognition. For the following analysis this appeal is made.[23]

Here Tillich seems to be making the paradoxical claim that there is a way to "verify" ontological judgments and yet there is not a way to argue for them. One must, it seems, simply present one's ontological judgments and see whether others agree with (or "recognize") them. I suppose Tillich would say that the wider the agreement, the more verified an ontological judgment is, or, speaking more individually, that an ontological judgment is verified for a given person when he agrees with it. But there is no way to prove the truth of, or argue for, an ontological assertion. One simply presents or expounds it. If the person "recognizes" it, no argument is necessary; if he does not, then apparently no argument is possible. So much, it would seem, for the question of the place of argument in ontology.

But we cannot stop here; we must at least restate this strange conclusion in order to feel the force of its strangeness. The key to verify to somebody that a given ontological assertion is true, one must attempt to gain his acceptance of that assertion, and to do this one can appeal only to his recognition of it. I suppose that one might phrase the assertion in various ways in an attempt to get him to "see" (or "feel") what one means, but no arguments would be relevant--any more than,

---

[23]Love, Power, and Justice, p. 24. Tillich also contrasts the experiential and the experimental in S.T., I, pp. 102ff.

say, arguments are usually held to be relevant to the "truth" of a poem. For example, suppose one wished to prove the truth of the typically Tillichian ontological judgment that all men are estranged from their essential being. There is apparently no way to prove this to an individual who disagreed. One could only clarify it by, perhaps, restating it in terms more familiar or intelligible to one's listeners. (This would be comparable to what we have called the apologetic or expressive function of dogma.) To a Christian one might translate the assertion by saying that all men are fallen. To somebody else one might say that no men are what they ought to be, or that men are against themselves, or that the human predicament is universal. But if the various attempts to gain recognition or agreement did not work, one would have to give up: no arguments seem available.

Thus when, in the Systematic Theology, Tillich is discussing the myth of the Fall or the "transition from essence to existence," he notes that he once heard a naturalistic philosopher say, "Man has no predicament."[24] But though Tillich calls such a denial self-deception,[25] he shows no way of convincing the naturalist of his error. Presumably, the naturalist could not argue for his view against the Christian, either. Each side is confronted with a fundamental difference in ways of seeing things, a fundamental disagreement over structures or presuppositions.

Indeed, Tillich even suggests that there could no more be an argument through which the Christian could convince the naturalist, or vice versa, than there could be an argument which would prove any theological assertion. Tillich seems to maintain that the fundamental presuppositions which a person holds are, by definition, theological. Thus both the denial as well as the acceptance of the doctrine of the Fall, according to Tillich, are matters of existential decision; they are matters of ultimate concern which "grasp" us but which we can only accept or reject, never prove.[26] This means that the naturalist is, in the broad sense, a theologian:

> If the idealist or naturalist asserts that
> "there is no human predicament," he makes an
> existential decision about a matter of ultimate

---

[24]S.T., II, p. 30.

[25]Ibid.

[26]We need not get into the problem of whether matters of ultimate concern are given or freely chosen. (Tillich's answer is that they are basically given, but in such a way that human freedom is not removed; i.e., we can accept or reject what is

> concern. In expressing his decision in con-
> ceptual terms, he is a theologian.[27]

We could state this in Tillichian terms by saying that all thinkers stand within some "theological circle."[28] And then we can express Tillich's apparently negative attitude toward settling issues by argument as follows: to the extent that their circles overlap, intelligent recognition is attainable and argument is unnecessary; but to the extent that they do not overlap, no recognition is attainable and argument is impossible.

This is what Tillich is getting at when he claims that theology and philosophy (ontology) are essentially and in principle united (though by no means identical), and that the philosopher differs from the theologian mainly in that his theology does and should remain hidden and implicit.[29]

And yet it is all very odd. For Tillich still claims that the philosopher, and the theologian insofar as he is a philosopher, must "argue for a philosophical opinion in the name of the universal logos and from the place which is no place: pure reason."[30] The philosophical basis for such argument, or, as Tillich says, such a "fight," is the "ontological analysis of the structure of being."[31]

What, if any, sense can we make of this? How can a fight between philosophers over the validity of ontological judgments be settled by arguments (from "pure reason"!) if nothing but the appeal to intelligent recognition is possible to evaluate ontological judgments? If I appeal to your intelligent recognition, I am not arguing, in any usual sense of that word. I am expounding or presenting or clarifying or "translating" or finding better words--but not arguing. I am not trying to show that you have made a logical error of some sort. And yet Tillich seems

---

given. Cf. Dynamics of Faith, pp. 1-8) The point is that whether one thinks of the "belief" in the Fall as a decision or as something given or as both, no arguments seem able to help ground the belief. One cannot prove that man is fallen.

[27] S.T., II, p. 30.

[28] S.T., I, pp. 8ff. This does not conflict with Tillich's claim that not everybody is in the theological circle, for he here means the Christian theological circle. Every man has an ultimate concern, therefore every man has a god, and therefore every man stands within some theological circle.

[29] Ibid., pp. 24ff.

[30] Ibid., p. 26.

[31] Ibid.

to hold that argument surely has its place in ontology. Does
Tillich contradict himself? Is argument possible or not? And if
it is possible, what kind of argument could it be?

Is there any way of rendering Tillich consistent and therefore "intelligible" here? I think there is, if we revert to our
usual method of attending not only to what Tillich says he does
but also to what he actually does. Let us, then, instead of
looking at Tillich's remarks about the possibility and (or) impossibility of arguing for fundamental ontological assertions, see
whether he himself argues for them, and if so, how he argues.

2. Contradictions in terms. There is a certain type of
argument Tillich uses which seems obviously to be relevant to
ontological disputes. These arguments, however, have something
odd about them. They do not seem to be strictly a type of deductive arguing; much less are they a type of inductive arguing--
though they seem to contain elements of both. These arguments, it
must be said, most closely resemble deductive arguments, but the
hidden presuppositions are usually so numerous that any number of
objections regarding the strict validity of the arguments, the
plausibility of the premises or especially the odd and unclear
definitions of the terms could be made. Yet Tillich himself seems
to see a certain necessity connecting his premises and conclusions.
It is as if he is suggesting that somehow the conclusions are
entailed by or contained in the premises--even though it is not
at all obvious that they are so contained.

Thus, for example, one of Tillich's arguments against the
supranaturalistic view of miracles is the following:

> If such an interpretation were true, the mani-
> festation of the ground of being would destroy
> the structure of being; God would be split within himself.[32]

That is, God as power would be split from God as Logos.
But the possible objections to this argument are countless.
Above all, it seems that Tillich is defining God as ground and
Logos, and then arguing against those who define God in another
way. What is the value of such an "argument?" How could it
succeed? To what would two theologians appeal in an attempt to
succeed? To what would two theologians appeal in an attempt to
settle the debate? No doubt they would appeal, in part, to
Christian Scripture and tradition--as Tillich does when he
defends his attempt to conceive God as Logos by referring to the
Logos Christology of some of the church fathers.[33] Would that
settle the issue? Of course not; Tillich's opponent would
refer, perhaps, to those church fathers who rejected the Logos

---

[32] Ibid., p. 116.   [33] Cf., e.g., Ibid., p. 157.

Christology. No doubt such debates can be interesting and infor-
mative, but can anything be settled this way? How can Tillich
suggest that there is some logical force to the argument, if it
depends on his own definition of God (and Logos, and ground)?
And even _if_ one accepts his definition, would it not be possible
to call God the Logos and yet believe in supranaturalistic miracles? Is there a contradiction here? Is it not difficult
enough to understand what Tillich means by terms like "Logos"?

Many examples of similarly puzzling arguments could be
given. Tillich often seems to argue that one assertion follows
from another when it seems apparent that only on his definition
of the terms could the argument be said to work--though it is
often still hard to see whether they work because clear definitions of the terms are seldom given. But instead of seeing many
of the other cases in which Tillich uses these odd arguments, I
wish to examine one particular exemplification of such argument
--for I think it is especially elucidatory of what may be going
on here.

Tillich sometimes argues against a given position that the
position is logically (or ontologically) impossible--or, as he
usually says, that it involves a "contradiction in terms." In
rejecting Aquinas' notion that there must be a kind of divine
existence that is not united with its essence, Tillich says:
"An existence of God which is not united with its essence is a
contradiction in terms."[34] Replying to a question by Charles
Hartshorne in _Philosophical_ _Interrogations_, he says that God
cannot be finite because "a 'finite' God is a contradiction in
terms."[35] Elsewhere he refers to the idea of an unconditioned
being as "a contradiction in terms."[36] Concerning the possibility of eternal condemnation, he states: "Logically this is
impossible to hold, because the very concept of the eternal
excludes being which is not in unity with love."[37] Again, he
states that "ontologically, eternal condemnation is a contradiction in terms,"[38] and once more, "if one speaks of everlasting
or endless condemnation, one affirms a temporal duration which

---

[34]_Ibid._, p. 236.

[35]Rome, p. 376.

[36]S.T., I, p. 207.

[37]_A_ _History_ _of_ _Christian_ _Thought_, p. 120.

[38]S.T., I, p. 285.

is not temporal. Such a concept is contradictory by nature."[39]
And in speaking of miracles, he says: "Jesus refuses to perform
'objective miracles.' They are a contradiction in terms."[40]

I would be inclined to suggest that this kind of argument
is fundamental to most of what seem to be Tillich's philosophical or ontological arguments, even where the words "contradiction in terms" do not occur. For Tillich sees existence as a
disruption of the essential nature of things,[41] and one might
say that what seems to be at stake in the above cases could be
phrased as questions of the nature or meaning or essence of God,
eternity, condemnation, and miracles. When Tillich argues
against "naturalists" such as Spinoza that man is finite freedom,[42] we can see him as saying that man is _essentially_ finite
and free, and it is possible to imagine Tillich saying that the
term "infinite man" or "unfree man" is a contradiction in terms
--i.e., that man would not _be_ man unless he were free and finite.
When Tillich says that Jesus' death and suffering are "necessary
consequences" of that which makes him the Christ,[43] we can again
see him as saying that a Jesus who did not suffer would not be
the Christ, or that a "non-suffering Christ" would be a contradiction in terms. And when Tillich says that naturalism or
rationalism, by depriving God of his abysmal element or power,
robs God of his divinity,[44] this could be phrased by saying that
a God without power is logically impossible or self-contradictory. In general, Tillich in his ontological judgments wants
to determine the essence or true nature of what he is discussing
and to show the way in which the essential becomes distorted.[45]

---

[39] Ibid., p. 284; cf. also S.T., III, p. 415, where Tillich
says that the concepts of eternity and death, "if taken at their
face value, are completely contradictory."

[40] S.T., I, p. 117.

[41] Cf., e.g., S.T., II, pp. 19-28.

[42] S.T., I, p. 237; S.T., II, p. 8; Rome, p. 384.

[43] S.T., II, p. 123.

[44] S.T., I, p. 251.

[45] For other examples of similar kinds of argument, cf. the
following: Dynamics of Faith, pp. 46-47, where Tillich says
that "the so-called existence of God is in itself an impossible
combination of words" and that therefore the question of the
existence of God is "meaningless"; S.T., I, pp. 204-205, where
he again refers to the impossibility of God's existence because
it "contradicts" the idea of a creative ground of essence and
existence; S.T., I, p. 247, where he says that if God is finite
"the divinity of God is undercut"; S.T., I, p. 248: "A condi-

Here Tillich's arguments <u>seem</u> deductive--that is, it would seem that one can at least determine, using the rules of deductive logic, what God, miracles, man, and so on are <u>not</u>. And the particular rule one uses is the principle of non-contradiction. But surely the matter is not this simple. Does Tillich really wish to maintain that those who believe in a being called God, in objective miracles, in human determinism, or in eternal condemnation are making the same sort of mistake as those who believe in square circles and married bachelors? And even if Tillich does wish to maintain such a silly thing, despite the odd fact that few if any people believe in married bachelors and yet great numbers believe in a being called God, in Hell, in determinism, and in miracles, is he also so naive that he does not see that such arguments will be futile in convincing his opponents--i.e., that in all probability it simple will not work to tell a fundamentalist that objective miracles are logically impossible? And why does Tillich not at least take the pains to try to show, instead of just state, that there is a contradiction in terms in such cases?

This whole issue is too strange and wondrous for me, and yet Tillich now and then makes some remarks which may clarify things. Consider, first, the following. In the dialogical book

---

tioned God is no God"; <u>S.T.</u>, II, p. 94: "The assertion that 'God became man' is not a paradoxical but a nonsensical statement" for as even the most consistent Scotists admitted, "the only thing that God cannot do is cease to be God"; <u>S.T.</u>, II, p. 174: "God would cease to be God" if he removed the destructive consequences of existential estrangement; <u>Love</u>, <u>Power</u>, <u>and</u> <u>Justice</u>, p. 114: God "has not the power to force somebody into his salvation. He would contradict himself. And this God cannot do"; <u>S.T.</u>, III, p. 284, where Tillich calls the divine mystery (the mystery of being) "the divinity of the divine"; <u>S.T.</u>, I, p. 272: "God's holiness . . . is that quality which qualifies all other qualities as divine"; <u>S.T.</u>, I, p. 250, where he says that the abysmal or power element in God "is the basis of Godhood, that which makes God God"; <u>S.T.</u>, I, p. 252: "The divine life and the divine creativity are not different. God is creative because he is God. Therefore, it is meaningless to ask whether creation is a necessary or contingent act of God. Nothing is necessary for God in the sense that he is dependent upon a necessity above him." (I wonder if we can compare the following to this last quotation: Circularity and roundless are not different. A circle is round because it is a circle. Therefore, it is meaningless to ask whether roundness is a necessary or contingent quality of circles. Roundness is not necessary for circles in the sense that they are dependent on a necessity above them--i.e., there is no strange power that forces all circles to be round.)

Ultimate Concern, someone asks Tillich whether miracles might
not be explained in terms of a "transcendent causality." Tillich's response is: "I would ask 'what does that mean,' because
I don't understand the combination of those two words."[46] Here
is a little food for thought. Tillich could perhaps have said
the same thing if he had said that the term "transcendent causality" is meaningless or a contradiction in terms. His further
remarks here indicate that this is so. He is clear enough about
the term "transcendent" and the term "causality," but he under-
stands the terms in such a way that they exclude one another--
what is transcendent transcends the realm of causality, and what
is causal is by definition something non-transcendent.

But Tillich here expresses himself rather mildly. He says
"I do not understand"; the suggestion seems to be that on his
own definition of the terms there is a contradiction, but he
leaves somewhat open the question whether his questioner might
have another definition of the terms which might make sense.
Here we might see Tillich not as arguing that "transcendent
causality" is simply meaningless, but merely stating (describing
the fact) that it is meaningless or not understandable to him.

It is as if a person did come up to me and say he saw a
square circle. I would really not be dismayed and wonder
whether, perhaps, he did; I would ask him what he is talking
about. I might even tell him that he is using improper English,
and I might refer him to various "authorities" on our language.
Unfortunately, terms like "transcendent," "God," "man," and
"miracle" are not so easily defined. Men disagree, and even
fight over, their definitions. And there's the rub. For then
one must be clear about which of the many possible definitions
one is using--and what better way to clarify oneself than by
saying, "On my definition of God, a finite God is a contradiction in terms." Is this, perhaps, what Tillich is saying with
all his "arguments" about logical impossibility?

But let us look further. What we seek are cases where
Tillich suggests that calling a phrase a contradiction in terms
is not a refutation but a clarification. In A History of Christian Thought, Tillich uses the concept of contradiction in
describing the thought of Socinus. He notes that according to
Socinus, man is free to sin or not sin. Each individual man
retains this freedom. Then Tillich says: "Hence, the idea of

---

[46]Brown, p. 162.

original or hereditary sin is a contradictory concept."[47]
Tillich is not here saying that the concept of original sin is
"really" contradictory, but that _for Socinus_ it was. It all
depends upon how one defines words like "sin." The point is that
here Tillich is simply clarifying the views of Socinus by saying
that according to him, "original sin" is a contradiction in
terms. He is saying that Socinus did not merely disbelieve in
the historical Adam and Eve and snake, but that he so defined
the term "sin" that whatever any ancestors of ours did, we cannot be held guilty for it.

In short, Tillich seems to be using the concept "contradiction in terms" in a relative sense. For a given speaker, with
certain definitions, certain word combinations are meaningless,
and it may be helpful in understanding that speaker if one sees
that and why they are meaningless or contradictory.

One other example can be given, one that is more relevant
to Tillich's own views. In _Philosophical Interrogations_, Charles
Hartshorne tries to argue, against Tillich, that literal language can be applied to God and that God must be considered finite.
Tillich responds, after noting his agreement with Hartshorne in
some respects, as follows:

> But in spite of my agreement with Hartshorne
> in these important points, I cannot accept his
> assertion that these elements which characterize
> finite being can be applied to God "literally,"
> because that would make God finite; and a "finite
> God" is a contradiction in terms.[48]

Here one would think that Tillich sees himself as having
offered a decisive rebuttal of all talk of a finite God. The
whole theory rests on a logical mistake, it would seem! But
Tillich's respect for Hartshorne, and Hartshorne's refusal to
mend his ways, indicate that Tillich's words here are misleading.
Surely Hartshorne cannot be so unintelligent as to have based
his whole theology on a contradiction in terms.

That much more is going on here than meets the eye is evident, I believe, from the fact that Tillich continues (I would
say "begins") his argument with Hartshorne _after_ saying that a
finite God is logically impossible. And he continues as
follows:

> If _this is denied_, he [God] becomes another
> name for the process of life, seen as a whole,
> and is subject to the tragic possibilities which

---

[47]_A History of Christian Thought_, p. 288.

[48]Rome, p. 376.

> threaten every finite process. Then not
> only is the world a risk taken by God, but
> God himself is a risk to himself, a risk
> which may fail.[49] (italics mine)

The words "If this is denied" are especially important here.
How could Hartshorne deny "this"--i.e., how could he rationally
deny that a finite God is a contradiction in terms? And yet
Tillich speaks as if it could be rationally denied, even though
he himself does not deny it. But must it not be the case that
"finite God" either is or is not a contradiction in terms?
Apparently not, for it depends upon what one means by "God."
One way to clarify what one means by God is to say that (for
oneself) a finite God is a contradiction in terms. The brunt of
Tillich's _argument_ is contained in the idea that a finite God is
a risk that may fail, not in the idea that such a God is logically impossible. The latter is a clarification, not (in this
context) an argument at all. It is neither intended as one by
Tillich nor would it be taken as one by Hartshorne. Hartshorne
would not try to "show" that his concept of a finite God is consistent (how would he show that?); he would try to deal with
Tillich's accusation that a finite God is subject to tragic
failure.

If, then, Tillich is using the phrase "contradiction in
terms" not as an argument or refutation but as a clarification
of his own meaning, many mysteries about his seeming philosophical arguments disappear. They are not, it would seem,
intended as arguments at all. Tillich _presupposes_ a certain
concept of God (and of eternity, miracle, etc.) according to
which certain things cannot be meaningfully said. We can see
these presuppositions or definitions (or presupposed definitions)
as constituting his basic ontological stance. But these presuppositions are not entirely clear: in particular, they will
tend to be "forgotten," since Tillich is giving rather unusual
definitions, or making unusual presuppositions, about God and
eternity and other objects of theological reflection. One way,
then, of reminding one's readers how such basic concepts are
being used is to show certain logically impossible or self-
contradictory ways of using them. Tillich would refuse to call
any existing thing by the name "God." He would refuse to call
an endless duration of suffering "eternal condemnation." He
would refuse to call an event which broke all possible laws of
nature a "miracle."

---

[49] _Ibid._

Of course, this is to suppose that a great part of Tillich's ontological and theological efforts are attempts to clarify rather than to substantiate his ontology. I do not know how I could prove this, but perhaps an experience of my own can provide some evidence. When I began to form the basic plan of this work, one of my main intentions was to see how Tillich argued by giving very careful attention to certain dialogical works where Tillich was forced to respond to questions. I felt I had to do this, since Tillich so seldom seemed to give clear or extensive arguments in his other works. But although I found much interesting material in these dialogical works, I was disappointed in two closely related ways.

In the first place, I found that most of the questions asked of Tillich were not criticisms (in the ordinary sense) but requests for clarification. They were of the form "What do you mean . . .?" Of course, such questions can be interpreted, and at least sometimes were intended, as criticisms, suggesting that perhaps Tillich meant nothing at all, or nothing of any clarity or import. But this is not how they were asked, and I think this is significant. It indicates that it is quite a common experience among readers of Tillich to be aware that they do not understand him, and thus that the first task, before any criticism or rebuttal or acceptance, is to clarify for themselves what he is saying. It is very much as if one of the major questions regarding Tillich is not whether his assertions are true but what they mean. If this is the case, and if Tillich was aware of it, we might expect him, in many of his assertions, not to be substantiating his ontology but to be clarifying it.

That the focus of Tillich's assertions is often more on clarification than proof can also be seen in the light of my second disappointment in reading Tillich's responses to questions. There still remained a considerable number of questions which were simply attacks: they were attempts to refute one of Tillich's views. It took, surprisingly, some time before I realized why Tillich's responses contained so little counter-argument. The basic answer I came to was the following: that Tillich responded to refutations by attempting to clarify himself. That is, he treated the criticism as based on a misunderstanding. One might say that whereas the one kind of questioner knew he did not understand and thus asked for help, the second thought he understood even though he did not, and thus his criticism was directed not against Tillich but against a misinterpretation of Tillich.

For example, Kai Nielsen attacks Tillich for attaching so much significance to ontological shock and the question which it generates, "Why is there something rather than nothing?"[50] Nielsen observes that there is no possible answer to this question which would not generate the same type of question. If "God" is the answer to the question why there is anything, then why is there a God? Tillich responds to this attack not by trying to show, as some Thomists might, that God is self-caused, but by stating that Nielsen missed the point. That is, Tillich does not take Nielsen's "criticism" as a criticism at all. He admits that the question, "Why is there something rather than nothing?" is not a proper question, i.e., it is not a question that can be answered. He also notes that he himself has often stated this. The question of non-being points to "that which precedes reason, . . . the merely given, the original fact."[51] In short, Tillich basically agrees with Nielsen (on this point), and the criticism arose from a misunderstanding.

The fact remains that Tillich sometimes does argue, and I have stated many of these arguments above (for example, the one against Hartshorne on the question of God's finitude). But the overwhelming impression is that Tillich sees his main task as that of clarifying and that his questioners in these dialogical works agree that indeed this should be his main task. One is even led to suspect that, for Tillich, arguments would cease if mutual understanding occurred. People might differ, but they would see that something other than argument, if anything at all, is needed to resolve ontological disputes.

But however much Tillich may be clarifying his own use of terms in his remarks about contradictions in terms and logical impossibility, there is something we have left out. Tillich does, after all, at least suggest that there is a certain incorrectness (and not just for himself) in speaking of God as a being. That is, Tillich is not merely giving his own "nominal" or personal or stipulative definition of God. He would somehow seek trans-personal backing for his definitions and concepts.

Tillich is no ordinary language philosopher. He does not appeal, for the "real" meaning of an elemental word, to the speech of ordinary men. He is quite aware that many ordinary men believe in (and therefore speak of) miracles and Hell and a being called God. But he thinks that these ordinary men, as

---

[50]Ibid., p. 403.

[51]Ibid., pp. 403-404.

well as the theologians who conceptualize their beliefs, are in
some sense wrong--and not just practically. And they are wrong
about the words and concepts which they themselves use. To what
does Tillich appeal for his own definitions or presuppositions?

Let us follow out Tillich's debate with Hartshorne. Tillich
says that if it is denied that a finite God is a contradiction
in terms (i.e., if the term God is being used in such a way that
God can be finite), then God is subject to the risk of failure.
In what sense can this be said to be an argument against Hartshorne, who might reply: so what? Is it an argument against
the existence of a finite God that he might fail? In his reply
to Hartshorne, Tillich does not clarify this. Peter Bertocci
apparently notices the fact, and asks much the same question as
we have indicated could be asked, namely, why it is "intolerable"
for God to be a risk to himself. Tillich's answer is the following:

> The reason I find "intolerable" the idea that
> God may be a risk to himself is that it contra-
> dicts the religious experience which is expressed
> in Psalm 90, or in the hymn which calls God the
> "rock of ages."[52]

This, of course, is not to be taken as a complete answer to
Bertocci (and Hartshorne), but points the direction in which
Tillich would go. He would appeal to that element in the Christian tradition which emphasizes the enduring power of God over
all tragic possibilities. It is a kind of appeal to experience,
except that it is not Tillich's own experience (nor the experience of "all men") but the experience of past Christians which
is decisive. That is to say, Tillich's concept of God is
derived, he thinks, from the Christian tradition. This tradition defines the word "God." And Tillich's argument against
Hartshorne is that he leaves something out of his concept of
God. We have previously dealt with such an argument.

But how could Hartshorne reply? He might reply that he is
not appealing to Christian tradition for his concept of God, in
which case there might be a stand-off of the sort one might find
between a Christian and a Hindu. Or Hartshorne might claim to
be within the Christian tradition, and he might justify this
claim by appealing to those parts of Scripture and tradition in
which God is explicitly or implicitly understood as finite. But
surely one would not expect to find decisive arguments here. We
have already reviewed the manifest difficulties in attempting to

---

[52]Ibid., p. 378.

settle disputes through an appeal to Scripture and tradition
(which still does not mean that Scripture and tradition are
irrelevant to such disputes).

The point here is that however Hartshorne would respond to
Tillich, the issue would ultimately rest upon how or from what
perspective or on the basis of what experiences one looked at
things, including Scripture and tradition. One's presuppositions
would again enter in as a source of the disagreement.

It is true that Tillich, in seeking the root meaning of
Christian symbols and concepts, often goes back to their original use, and (like Heidegger) he does the same with elemental
words of the philosophical tradition. But however much he might
think that ontological analysis must involve such inquiries into
the original power of words, neither Tillich nor Heidegger would
claim (despite the etymologies both attempt) that such matters
can be settled by argument. Much more would depend upon a certain feel for the words. And what is significant in our context
is that people feel toward such elemental words many different
ways. How does one determine when one has gotten an adequate
interpretation? And may there not be, as in poetry, many possible interpretations? May these many possible interpretations
not be part of the depth of Scripture and tradition, allowing
them to speak to so many people at so many different times?

But Tillich still seems to be interested in "the" real
meaning of terms like "God" and "justice." And somehow arguments seem to be relevant, even though the arguments would have
to be arguments over presuppositions. We must look further if
we wish to find a form of argument which might be relevant to the
solution of ontological disputes.

3. Arguments regarding presuppositions. Is there any way
of settling disputes over presuppositions? How could there be,
since one would have to appeal to something prior to the presuppositions themselves? But if there is no way, then it would
seem that reason (in the sense of rational argument) cannot
settle ontological disputes. But this is most odd, since most
ontologists claim that they are being extremely rational, and
we have seen that one of the main points of ontology is to help
settle conflicts by seeking root meanings.

Let us also remember that Tillich himself seems to assert
both sides of this paradox. We have seen that he holds that
ontological assertions can be verified only by intelligent
recognition, but that he also holds that they can be argued
for (fought over) on the basis of pure reason, in the name of

the universal logos. Does Tillich give any arguments which
would make sense of such assertions?

We have already noted that Tillich comments on the conflict
between Christians on the one hand and naturalists and idealists
on the other regarding man's predicament (the Fall). He seems
to suggest that no arguments can be given which would be relevant to the dispute, since the dispute is ultimately "theological." But let us look more closely, and again not at what
Tillich says is possible but what he actually does. Does
Tillich ever present any arguments against the naturalists and
idealists who deny the Fall? Sometimes he seems to. For example, he charges Spinoza with denying human freedom,[53] he charges
Stoicism with leading to resignation or apathy or cynicism,[54]
and he charges Hegel with identifying revelation with ontological
reason.[55]

But can we call these arguments? That is, could they con-
ceivably function as arguments? Could they help to persuade, or
to settle a "fight?" Would we expect a naturalist or idealist
to see the error of his ways upon being confronted with Tillich's
"arguments"? Surely not. For Spinoza would happily admit that
he denies freedom (in Tillich's sense), the Stoic might not only
admit that Stoicism leads to apathy but might strongly assert
that the attainment of true resignation or impassibility or
apathy (apatheia) is the whole point of the Stoic system,[56] and
Hegel would no doubt admit that he identifies nearly everything
with its seeming opposite, including revelation and ontological
reason. Thus we might say that Tillich is not really giving an
argument here, but only presenting the difference between Christian theology, on the one hand, and naturalism and idealism on
the other. Christianity, he might be saying, demands the rejection of, for example, Stoic resignation or Spinozistic determinism. And it demands such rejection because it "sees" what
it considers practical dangers, a host of destructive conse-

---

[53]S.T., I, p. 237.

[54]S.T., II, p. 30; The Courage to Be, p. 24.

[55]S.T., I, p. 74.

[56]That a Stoic might even accept the label "cynical" is
made plausible by the fact that the Greek Stoics are usually
considered to have grown out of the previous school called the
Cynics, whence the word cynicism derives.

quences, in such views.

But let us consider this matter more carefully. I suppose
that one could see real arguments here, depending upon to whom
Tillich's remarks are addressed, or, in other words, depending
upon just what the point of Tillich's remarks is. For Tillich
may not be trying to convince the naturalist that he is wrong
in, say, denying human freedom but to convince the Christian that
it is wrong ("unchristian") to deny human freedom. That is,
Tillich may simply be trying to argue that Christianity is not
compatible with naturalism, since Christianity asserts (or presupposes) the reality of freedom. The naturalists or idealists,
for their part, might wish to argue the same thing--as Spinoza,
for example, surely would. But they might not, too: we think
for example of Kierkegaard's attack upon Hegel not only for overlooking the reality of freedom and sin and revelation but
especially for claiming that such views correspond to the inmost
essence of Christianity.

Thus we might see one of Tillich's tasks as a theologian as
the task of bringing out the ontological presuppositions of
Christianity in order to more sharply distinguish Christianity
from what it is not. Tillich would then be seen as arguing not
against the thoroughgoing naturalist or idealist (with whom
Tillich differs but cannot argue) but with the Christian naturalist (or naturalistic Christian). And to him Tillich's basic
argument would be either that such a person is not sufficiently
comprehensive (of Christian Scripture and tradition: i.e., that
he leaves something out) or that such a person is inconsistent
(i.e., that he includes the various elements in Christianity but
in such a way that he contradicts himself). And as we have seen,
the Church would take an interest in such a lack of comprehensiveness or consistency because of the dangerous consequences which
are the usual result.

There might, of course, also be an apologetic purpose in
arguing against those who overlook the deep differences between
Christianity and naturalism, if one were speaking to those who
already reject naturalism. The effect of arguing that Christianity and naturalism are incompatible might be to make such
people attend more carefully to the Christian message than they
would if they thought (as they might if they had been reading
certain liberal theologians) that Christianity and naturalism
fundamentally agree.

We could also take note of the other side of each of these
coins: the apologetic and protective function of showing the
extent to which, despite basic differences, there are basic

similarities between Christianity and other views. But we can
stop here. For we have not only returned to points we have
already made, but we have also strayed from our path. Our intent
was to see whether Tillich has any arguments which might be relevant to the thoroughgoing naturalist himself. What about the
person who claims that there has been no Fall, that there is no
human predicament, without also claiming that this belief is
consistent with Christianity? Can the Christian theologian not
only disagree (differ) with him but also fruitfully argue with
him? Or is it all a matter of intelligent recognition, existential decision, and historical destiny?

Perhaps a clue can be found on the very pages in the Systematic Theology where Tillich criticizes the naturalistic and
idealistic rejection of the Fall.[57] So far as I can see, he
does not there present an argument which a Christian theologian
might use against a naturalist.[58] But he does suggest one which
an idealist might use against a naturalist, and it is a most
interesting argument. To find and understand it, let us more
carefully attend to Tillich's discussion.

Tillich first points out that "idealism as well as naturalism stand against the Christian (and Platonic) symbol of the
Fall."[59] (Let us overlook this implicit but odd distinction
between Platonism and idealism; the idealists Tillich here has
in mind are exemplified by the Hegelians. Tillich is rather
inconsistent in his use of terms like "idealism" and "naturalism,"
and his meaning at any time must be derived from the particular
context). According to the idealists of whom Tillich is speaking
here, the Fall is, so to speak, not taken seriously enough: for
them, "the Fall is not a break, but an imperfect fulfillment."[60]
That is, the Fall is seen to be necessary for the sake of something better, and thus it was not a really tragic happening at
all. Tillich distinguishes two forms of what he calls "the
idealist faith": the progressivistic (or revolutionary) and the
conservative. He claims that Christianity and existentialism
consider the former as utopianism, the latter as ideology, and
both as self-deception and idolatry. "Neither takes the self-
contradicting power of human freedom and the demonic implications

---

[57]S.T., II, pp. 29-30.

[58]Except very indirectly--but we will come to that.

[59]S.T., II, p. 29. The existentialists, Tillich later suggests, are on the side of the Christians and Platonists (p. 30).

[60]Ibid., p. 30.

of history seriously."[61]

So far Tillich has not presented any clear argument of the
type we seek. At most he shows, or vaguely suggests, how
Christianity and idealism differ. But could any of Tillich's
remarks be expected to alter the views of the idealist? I do
not see how. An idealist might freely admit that he was utopian,
he might ask what on earth Tillich means by ideology and what is
wrong with it, he might ask Tillich to show exactly how idealism
deceives itself, he might wonder what relevance to him the
charge of idolatry has, and he might happily admit to his denial
of human freedom and the demonic, at least in Tillich's sense of
these terms.

What about naturalism, then? Does Tillich forward any arguments against it? Tillich states that naturalism denies the
Fall, or the transition from essence to existence, "from the
other side, so to speak."[62] What Tillich seems to be getting at
is that whereas the idealist might use the concept of estrangement (or the symbol of the Fall), albeit in a watered-down form,
the naturalist rejects the concept altogether. The naturalist
takes existence for granted; he urges resignation and suggests
we are foolish to worry about or contend with the so-called
negativities of life. I suppose that Tillich's naturalists
would claim that evil is "all in the mind" or that it has no
objective reality, and thus that it is something that can best
be met by not attending to it or not worrying about it--i.e., by
simple resignation or a thoroughgoing attitude of Stoicism.

The strange ontological and semantic difficulties one gets
into in making sense of what the naturalist says (or what Tillich says he says) are not to the point. What is interesting is
the criticism which Tillich directs against the naturalist, a
criticism essentially different from his criticisms of idealism.
He does not simply portray the differences between Christianity
and naturalism, suggesting how the naturalist is to be regarded,
by the Christian, as not "intelligently recognizing" his ideolo-
gical, idolatrous, and self-deceptive errors. Instead Tillich
says the following:

> Naturalists, however, usually avoid resignation
> or cynicism by including elements of idealism
> either in their progressivistic form or in the
> more realistic form of Stoicism. In both forms,
> pure naturalism is transcended, but the symbol

---

[61] Ibid.

[62] Ibid.

of the Fall is not reached. This is not even achieved in ancient Stoicism's belief in the deterioration of man's historical existence and in the gap between the fools and the wise ones. Neo-Stoicism is impregnated with so many idealistic elements that it does not reach the full depth of Christian realism.[63] (italics mine)

I believe that this passage contains, for the first time, a potentially effective argument. What Tillich suggests is that in fact few people really are naturalists, however much they may claim to be. That is, however much they may claim that man has no predicament, they do not really believe this; in their speaking or writing or acting they indicate that they presuppose at least as much of a predicament as the idealist does.

What point can we make here? I believe that we now have an argument which the idealist might use against the naturalist in an ontological dispute. For if what Tillich says is true, then an idealist might argue with a naturalist by saying: you do not maintain your position; you presuppose idealism even though you say you deny it.[64] To use good existentialist and Tillichian terminology, the charge is one of self-deception;[65] or to use Platonic and again Tillichian terminology, the charge is one of forgetting, of not remembering or recollecting or recognizing what one in fact believes or presupposes.

I think that this is a type of argument which we have not previously analyzed. This argument must not be confused with the previously discussed arguments which have to do with comprehensiveness and consistency. Though there are similarities, there are very important differences. The consistency at stake here is not consistency in principle; it might be possible to have a consistent naturalism. Tillich's point is that it is usually not the case that a given naturalist is consistent with himself, and when it is not the case, or insofar as it becomes sufficiently obvious that it is not the case, a philosophical or ontological argument can occur.

---

[63]Ibid.

[64]The Christian theologian might also use this argument against naturalism, as Tillich himself obviously does, but it would serve only to make the naturalist admit that he was, in part, an idealist, not a Christian. Of course, if idealism were objectionable to him for other reasons, then he might, I suppose, listen to Christianity.

[65]That it may be possible to show this in the case of most idealists is perhaps what Tillich meant when he accused idealism of self-deception.

Somebody, perhaps Bertrand Russell, is supposed to have
said that scepticism is in principle the most consistent philosophical position, but that in fact nobody has ever been a
sceptic. The suggestion may have been that the easiest way to
refute somebody who claims to be a sceptic is to show him that
however consistent he may be in principle, he is not in fact a
sceptic and deceives himself if he claims to be. It is this
kind of argument with which we are concerned here.

Of course, I hardly wish to rest my case for a "new" type
of argument, one which moreover is, for Tillich, especially
relevant to philosophical or ontological disputes, on this one
example. Tillich continually makes use of such an argument. For
instance, we have seen above that he criticizes pragmatism for
not being aware that a principle is needed with which to determine whether a hypothesis "works" or is successful. The pragmatist, we might say, claims to have only a pragmatic criterion,
but according to Tillich he "deceives himself" by presupposing a
more fundamental criterion[66]--and the important point here is
that, if this is true, an argument with the pragmatist is possible. One can attempt to show him that he himself uses non-
pragmatic criteria.

We can also refer here to Tillich's remarks on Freud's
inconsistency. As we have seen, Tillich holds that Freud was
not entirely clear about his ontological presuppositions: at
times he presupposed that man is essentially and thus inevitably
estranged, and at times he held that man could be healed. We
have already seen the consequences that Tillich thinks followed
from this inconsistency, namely, that it led his followers to
drop one of the sides of the contradiction, and with it an important insight into human nature. We used this as an analogy to
clarify why Tillich thinks inconsistencies in religious thought
are dangerous. But how would Tillich argue with Freud himself?
How can a Christian theologian, using an ontology expressing
the fundamental presuppositions of the Christian faith, argue
against one who had a different ontology?

This issue becomes especially perplexing in view of the
fact that Tillich claims to be able to offer a "basic theological
criticism" of Freud's doctrine of man.[67] What can this mean?
How, and to what end, does a Christian theologian offer criticisms of non-Christians. That is, what makes him think that the

---

[66]S.T., I, p. 150.

[67]Theology of Culture, p. 119.

non-Christian will listen? Why should he listen, if his presuppositions about reality differ from that of the Christian theologian? What results could I expect if I criticized an atheist's immoral actions by saying to him that such actions are against the will of God? Tillich seems to be saying that Christianity has three fundamental doctrines: the doctrine of the goodness of creation, the doctrine of the Fall, and the doctrine of Salvation,[68] and that the theologian can criticize Freud for not accepting these. But surely, it would seem, the theologian, in claiming that Freud does not accept all these doctrines, cannot be said to be expressing a _criticism_ of Freud but only a _difference_ with Freud. As criticism, his remarks would seem to have no logical force at all.

How then _can_ the theologian criticize someone else? So far as I can see, there is only one way, and this is perhaps how Tillich intends his remarks on Freud to be taken. The Christian theologian can try to show that Freud presupposes what he claims to deny: the need for an ultimate hope in something outside of man. Freud's inconsistency prevented him from seeing his own presupposition. Freud did have a "religious" (in the broad sense) hope, but he was not aware of it.

Tillich also uses this type of argument when arguing against an exclusively personalistic concept of God. Again one seems to be confronted with an impasse: Tillich presupposes one view (or definition) of God and the personalist presupposes another. How can argument take place? None can, perhaps, if Tillich is speaking to a _thoroughgoing_ personalist. But what if there are far fewer thoroughgoing personalists than one thinks? What if personalists themselves presuppose that God is more than a person? Then argument can take place. Thus Tillich tries to point out things that the personalist himself says, or else things (from Scripture, say) which he would accept, in which the personalist seems to move beyond mere personalism.

For example, Tillich shows a way of arguing with a Lutheran personalist by showing that he himself is not aware of the transpersonalism he presupposes.

> Luther, who was very suspicious of philosophy, speaks of God as being nearer to all creatures than they are to themselves, or of God being totally present in a grain of sand and at the same time not being comprehended by the totality of all things, or of God giving the power to the arm of the murderer to drive home the murderous

---

[68] _Ibid._, pp. 118-119.

knife. Here Luther's sometimes unreflective
biblical personalism is transcended, and God
as the power of Being in everything is ontologically affirmed.[69]

This is also how we can interpret Tillich's remarks about
the element of doubt in every faith, and the element of faith in
every doubt.[70] If one were confronted with the simple situation
that some people have a thoroughgoing attitude of faith and others
a thoroughgoing attitude of doubt, no arguments could, apparently,
be relevant. But Tillich seems to think that such cases are more
rare than we think. Even the man of faith will often admit he
cannot "possess" God, that he cannot know for certain. And even
the man who doubts still commits himself to something; he has an
ultimate concern, a "god." In these cases, then, one could try
to argue with each of these men if they were at odds with one
another, showing them that they are in fact not as much at odds
as would appear.

In A History of Christian Thought, Tillich utilizes a similar argument against Harnack and Barth. He accuses them of a
kind of Marcionism.[71] He suggests that their negative attitude
toward the created world is fundamentally the same as that which
inspired the Marcionite distinction between the God of creation
and the God of salvation. Of course, this argument would have
no possible effect if, say, Barth accepted Marcion. But he obviously does not; he sees its danger, and in seeing the relation
between his view and Marcion's he may be led to see that his own
view is similarly dangerous.

Again, Tillich argues in a similar way against the view of
kerygmatic (as opposed to apologetic) theologians like Barth that
theology should not use philosophical or "situational" concepts
in speaking the message, for fear of losing the message of
kerygma. One of Tillich's arguments here is that such an approach
is illegitimate: "it does not fulfill the aim of the theological
function of the church." This seems to mean that there are certain dangerous consequences in such an attitude. But according

---

[69]Biblical Religion and the Search for Ultimate Reality,
p. 84; cf. also Rome, pp. 380-381, where Tillich gives a similar
argument against Thielicke's personalism.

[70]Biblical Religion and the Search for Ultimate Reality,
pp. 58-62; cf. also Dynamics of Faith, pp. 20-22.

[71]A History of Christian Thought, p. 34; cf. also S.T., I,
p. 155, where Tillich accuses those theologians (presumably the
neo-orthodox) who reject reason of showing Manichean traits.

to whom are they <u>dangerous</u> consequences? Perhaps not to the
kerygmatic theologian, given <u>his</u> presuppositions. But Tillich
adds another argument:

> And, beyond all this, it is impossible.
> Even kerygmatic theology must use the
> conceptual tools of its period. It cannot
> simply repeat biblical passages. Even
> when it does, it cannot escape the conceptual
> situation of the different biblical writers.[72]

The point is that <u>in fact</u> the kerygmatic theologian <u>does</u> use
philosophical, cultural, or situational concepts, whether he
wishes to be aware of it (or admit it) or not.

> The fundamentalist minister who said to me
> "Why do we need philosophy when we possess
> all truth through revelation?" did not
> realize that in using the words "truth" and
> "revelation," he was determined by a long
> history of philosophical thought which gave
> these words the meaning in which he used
> them. We cannot avoid philosophy, because
> the ways we take to avoid it are carved out
> and paved by philosophy.[73]

And Tillich notes that a theologian like Barth, despite his
criticism of those who (like Tillich) construct a theology which
responds to the contemporary situation, in fact does the same
himself:

> Barth's greatness is that he corrects himself
> again and again in the light of the "situation"
> and that he strenuously tries not to become his
> own follower. Yet he does not realize that in
> doing so he ceases to be a merely kerygmatic
> theologian.[74]

It is interesting to note how this last "criticism" is
p hr ased. For of course it could happen that the more Tillich
emphasizes the inconsistency between what Barth says and what he
does, the more Barth would respond by being careful <u>not</u> to respond to the situation. But this is not at all what Tillich
wants; if that were the effect of his argument, he would probably
not use the argument at all for fear of making things worse
instead of better. Thus Tillich does not couch the argument in
the form of a criticism of Barth, but as praise of Barth:
"Barth's greatness is that he corrects himself again and again."
One must be careful with these arguments; they are so powerful
that they may backfire. We shall return to this point.

---

[72]<u>S.T.</u>, I, p. 7.

[73]<u>Biblical Religion and the Search for Ultimate Reality</u>,
p. 10.

[74]<u>S.T.</u>, I, p. 5.

To note but a few other examples, Tillich often criticizes Protestantism in the name of the Protestant principle.[75] He criticizes those, like the humanists, who reject everything religious for not realizing that their own answers to man's problems come from religious sources.[76] He criticizes the logical positivists who claim to have no ontology by saying that they deceive themselves: their own assertions presuppose ontological judgments.[77] As we have already seen, he replies to those who reject systematic consistency not only by showing the legitimacy and value of consistency, but by pointing out that his critics themselves desire consistency: "It often happens that those who attack the systematic form are very impatient when they discover an inconsistency in someone else's thought."[78]

Thus our original dilemma, whether ontological disputes can be settled by intelligent recognition or by argument, is seen to be false. The answer is both: one uses that type of argument which aims at making one's opponent recognize for himself that he presupposes what he seems to deny.

This is what Tillich means when he says that apologetic theology, i.e., for Tillich, ontological theology, "presupposes common ground,"[79] and that "it is the task of apologetic theology to prove that the Christian claim also has validity from the point of view of those outside the theological circle."[80] It is, one might say, Tillich's belief that men do share this common ground, that they in fact agree upon their fundamental presuppositions. But these presuppositions, just like faith itself, are in a kind of tension, a creative tension which becomes split due to the intrusion of demonic elements.

We can also note that here the theoretical and the practical merge. The practical issues presuppose a certain stance toward theoretical ones, but the most theoretical issues of all, the ontological ones, are ultimately the most practical of all. The aim of ontology, or of an ontological theology, is to drive toward reunion, i.e., its aim is love. The ultimate standard

---

[75]Cf., e.g., Theology of Culture, p. 138; S.T., III, p. 239.

[76]S.T., II, p. 26; cf. also Theology of Culture, p. 125.

[77]S.T., I, p. 20.

[78]Ibid., p. 58; cf. also Kegley and Bretall, p. 330.

[79]S.T., I, p. 6.

[80]Ibid., p. 15.

determining the apologetic and protective functions of theology
is love,[81] and it is precisely this which is the legitimate
power behind ontology. The criterion of love is identical with,
or rather "love" for the Christian is defined by, the one positive doctrine in Christianity, "the ultimate criterion of all
revelatory experiences--the New Being in Jesus as the Christ."[82]

I wish to make, however, one more point regarding the kind
of argument we have been discussing. Despite the above examples
of Tillich's use of arguments from presuppositions, there remains
a rather odd fact, namely, that he does not explicitly use them
as much as we might expect. By interpreting his remarks, we can
often find them present, but Tillich does not make as much use of
them as, in principle, he should. For given that Tillich is
right that there is always a common ground and thus room for argument, then there would seem to be unlimited potential for using
it. But I cannot find nearly as many examples of Tillich's use
of this kind of argument as I could find examples of his other
types of argument--arguments having to do, ultimately, with the
apologetic and protective results of speaking in a certain way.
And yet in the final analysis any hope for agreement by way of
argument seems to rest upon bringing people, inside and outside
the church, to agreement over their presuppositions. Why does
Tillich then not pay far closer attention to the one kind of
argument which might work?

Frankly, I do not know why he doesn't. But there are two
possible answers, I suppose: first, that he has the arguments
but desires not to use them, and second, that he does not really
have them. Let us consider the first possibility. For it could
be maintained that arguing with somebody, especially over very
"deep" or existential issues, is simply not the best way to convince him. While it is true that arguing with somebody can be
seen as the attempt to make him consider things he had not considered, as an attempt, in short, to open him to some new possibilities already somehow present in him, it is also true that
arguing can be seen, or felt, as an attempt to force the other
into one's own position, as an attempt to dominate him. Surely
Tillich would accept the insights of Freud, Nietzsche, and Paul
that we are not as rational or neutral or sinless as we think we

---

[81]S.T., III, pp. 125, 154. One should say "faith and love,"
but the two are actually but two sides of the same ecstatic state
of being. (Ibid., pp. 129, 135)

[82]Ibid., p. 128.

are. We all realize, I suppose, that there are times when we argue with somebody not for the sake of leading him to a truth which may be beneficial to him and to humanity, but rather to triumph over him. Perhaps more often, we realize that others are arguing with us for that reason. And such a situation, or even the possibility of it, could destroy the whole point of arguing in the first place.

If I inform someone that he has contradicted himself, perhaps informing him of this with a touch of glee, he may grudgingly admit it. But he will probably fight back. At most he may give up one of his mutually inconsistent assertions, and it is not unlikely that he will give up the one I wished him to retain, holding on resolutely to the one I thought was most dangerous. Such a consequence could hardly be said to serve the purpose of my argument.

Suppose I am confronted by a Nazi who claims that all Jews are evil. And suppose I remind him that his friend, whom he dearly loves, is Jewish, thus employing a form of the argument we have been discussing. "You cannot consistently maintain," I might say, "that all Jews are evil and that your Jewish friend is good." The consequences may be disastrous; instead of opening him to the possibility that, like any other men, Jews must be judged (if at all) individually, I may lead him to resolve the inconsistency by giving up his friend.

The point here is that most of Tillich's arguments can be easily dodged; any number of possible answers can be given. There is a _looseness_ to them, something dependent upon personal opinion, weight of evidence, and (ultimately) presuppositions, and this looseness prevents them from forcing even the most rational opponents into agreement. Perhaps this is as it should be. But the type of argument we have been examining is different: to be caught with one's presuppositions askew is to be caught in a state of dishonesty or self-deception. The argument is a particularly _embarrassing_ one. This may partially explain why Tillich uses the argument in its most explicit form only sparingly, and against positions which would radically undercut simply everything he stands for (such as the neo-orthodox rejection of apologetic theology).

But there may be a second reason why Tillich does not use such arguments, namely, that he does not have them. For I doubt that we need think that Tillich is so logically astute as to have at his disposal compelling arguments against everybody else and that he does not use them simply because he feels he ought not.

136

For one thing, Tillich emphasizes that however much he agrees
with Hegel that truth is the whole, he is against him with
respect to his apparent belief that he had managed, at least in
principle, to grasp the whole.[83] A position such as Hegel's
leads to the rejection as false or irrational of insights which
do not fit one's system and especially to a shutting oneself to
new experiences. This means that Tillich must listen as carefully to others as he wishes others to listen to him.

But there is more to this matter, for I rather suspect that
there is something about the type of argument we have been looking
at which makes it in principle impossible for it decisively to
succeed--especially in a published work. For one is never quite
certain that one's opponent has contradicted himself, simply
because one is never quite certain what he means. These arguments must, to be most valid and effective, operate on an individual level. To argue against "naturalism" may be to be arguing
against nobody at all, at least none of one's readers. And even
when Tillich argues against Barth, is he quite sure what Barth
intends when he speaks against the use of philosophical concepts?
Perhaps the argument regarding presuppositions can be used best
only against individuals in discussions with them, where there
is the opportunity for mutual clarification. Perhaps Plato was
right in seeing the essence of philosophy as lying in personal,
mutual questioning, in dialogue of a sort. Still nearer the mark
may have been Socrates, who engaged in dialogues rather than
writing them. It often seems true, in any case, that the arguments most often advanced in philosophy and theology against
other men's positions seem aimed at straw men, once one familiar-
izes oneself with the thinkers under attack.

This may help explain the odd fact that exactly those arguments which Tillich uses the most are the ones that are least
rigorous, and the one argument which remains, the one that could
be used in the most rigorous way, is least often put in the form
of an argument. The point is that rigor, when arguing not over
scientific theories but over existential problems, may be of no
great value. I strongly suspect that this is why Tillich prefers
to present his theology, hoping that it will call forth recognition and keeping the argumentative character of it implicit,
rather than adopt the polemical alternative of carefully picking
apart the views of his opponents. At their deepest levels, the
whole concept of "argument" and the correlative concept of

_____

[83]Ibid., p. 255.

"opponents" become ambiguous at best, outrightly destructive at worst. Seeing truth as a matter of argument and the world as consisting of opponents is, while an existential fact, also something we hope to overcome. Such, I think, is involved in Tillich's view of things.

D. Ontology, Theology, and Truth

What, after all this, can we say about truth? Does theology, even ontological theology, give us access to an otherwise inaccessible kind of truth? Are we supposed to discover something about the nature of reality itself, or about being itself, by reading Tillich's theology? And if we do discover some kind of truth, how does such truth serve the church? It has become obvious that in some sense the question of the truth content of an ontological theology depends upon the prior question of the truth content of ontology itself. Thus we can ask, and have attempted to ask in this chapter, what is the nature and function of ontology. But the attempt to answer this question has led us into a concept of ontology centered around man, his insights, and his ethical responsibilities. Ontology seems to be the attempt to render consistent the fundamental insights or presuppositions of man: it is the attempt to be consistent and comprehensive. An ontological analysis of a particular problem, say the problem of justice, is the attempt to render consistent man's fundamental insights regarding justice. But when we asked the question of the verification of ontology, we found that Tillich's answer did not allow us to transcend the realm of the phenomenal, the realm of the merely apparent or encountered reality (i.e., reality as men see it). Ontology can be verified only by intelligent recognition. We saw that this still leaves room for arguing or debating about different ontological views. Since ontology has to do with insights or presuppositions, the type of argument most appropriate to ontology consists in showing one's opponent that he deceives himself, or that he presupposes at one point what he denies at another.

But what has all this to do with truth? Do men necessarily come nearer to the truth, in the strictly theoretical sense, the more nearly they are able to bring together or render consistent their basic insights? Are the insights themselves necessarily true, and if so, are they somehow more true (or true in another sense) when they are brought into consistent relation with other insights? What makes Tillich so sure that these insights, coherently ordered, are true?

The key to understanding Tillich here has to do with seeing

138

what he means by "truth." This is no easy task, and I shall
allow myself only such remarks as bring to some end, however
vague, our preceding discussion of Tillich's ontology. Tillich
is, to me at least, simply not entirely clear about the whole
issue of truth, in particular, conceptual (or rational or philosophical) truth. Conceptual truth seems to be such an obvious
good to him that he seldom asks just in what that good consists.
Perhaps he was more taken by the grandeur and beauty of the history of philosophy, especially in its most speculative and metaphysical forms, than are many of his readers, I for one. At any
rate, my remarks on Tillich's concept of truth must be judged
largely on the basis of the sense it makes of the preceding.

Tillich's discussion of truth in the Systematic Theology is
enlightening only up to a point. He decisively rejects any
attempt to restrict the use of the predicate "true" to analytic
propositions and experimentally confirmed ones.[84] This is "a
simple semantic device," but it would mean "a break with the
whole Western tradition," necessitating "the creation of another
term for what has been called alethes or verum in classical,
ancient, medieval, and modern literature."[85]

Rather, truth is a matter of penetrating beneath the surface
of things, for "things hide their true being."[86] Tillich then
claims that "this notion of truth is not bound to its Socratic-
Platonic birthplace,"[87] and in apparent support of this he
attempts to explain the universal origin of the notion of truth.

> One could say that the concept of true being
> is the result of disappointed expectations in
> our encounter with reality. . . . The truth
> of something is that level of its being the
> knowledge of which prevents wrong expectations
> and consequent disappointments.[88]

This is the notion of truth we might expect in the light of
Tillich's very practical apologetic and protective criteria for
judging theological assertions. It is also the notion of truth
we might expect from a thoroughgoing pragmatist. But we have
seen in this chapter that Tillich is not a thoroughgoing pragmatist; he thinks that pragmatism needs ontological foundations.

---

[84]S.T., I, p. 100.

[85]Ibid.

[86]Ibid, p. 101.

[87]Ibid.

[88]Ibid., pp. 101-102.

With respect to the quotation above, we can say that Tillich does
not clarify how one knows what to count as a "wrong" expectation,
and especially how one knows that human expectations have anything to do with ultimate reality or true being.

Can we get further light by examining other places in which
he deals with this issue? Sometimes he attaches special significance to the etymology of the word "truth," or rather the etymology of the Greek equivalent, "aletheia." In one of the essays
in The Protestant Era, he observes that "alethes, in Greek, means
'not hidden.' Knowing the truth means penetrating to that level
of reality which is hidden to the natural world view and can be
discovered only by methodological knowledge."[89] In another essay
in the same volume, he says much the same:

> The meaning of being manifests itself in the
> logos of being, that is, in the rational word
> that grasps and embraces being and in which
> being overcomes its hiddenness, its darkness,
> and becomes truth and light. Truth in Greek
> is aletheia, "what is not hidden." In the
> word--the logos--being ceases to be hidden; in
> the rational form being becomes meaningful and
> understandable.[90]

What does all this mean? It becomes rather difficult at
this point for me to see how philosophical aletheia is different
from revelation, which Tillich defines in the Systematic Theology
as "a special and extraordinary manifestation which removes the
veil from something which is hidden in a special and extraordinary way."[91] When something becomes true it becomes unhidden;
when something becomes revealed the "veil" is removed from it.
But surely there is a difference between conceptual (or philosophical) truth and revealed truth.

A rather off-hand remark about the revelatory and the conceptual in the last volume of the Systematic Theology may shed
some light here. Tillich is dealing with his doctrine of Eternal
Life, or the transition from the temporal to the eternal, and he
notes the difficulty in clarifying this concept. Numerous questions can be asked about it. How can they be answered? Tillich
replies as follows:

> Such questions can only be answered in the
> context of a whole system as implications
> of main concepts (being, non-being, essence,
> existence, finitude, estrangement, ambiguity,

---

[89]The Protestant Era, p. 30.

[90]Ibid, p. 90.

[91]S.T., I, p. 108.

and so on) as well as of the central religious
symbols (creation, the Fall, the demonic,
salvation, agape, Kingdom of God, and so on).
Otherwise, the answers would be mere opinions.
flashes of insight, or mere poetry (with its
revealing but non-conceptual power).[92] (italics
mine)

Here Tillich suggests that poetry has revelatory but not
conceptual power. But does poetry give a kind of non-conceptual
truth? Tillich does not wish to argue that we need use the word
"truth" in such a way, although he is aware that it is possible
to do so. When he deals with the question of the nature of
aesthetic creativity, he wavers on the issue:

The intention of finding truth is only one
element in the aesthetic function. The main
intention is to express qualities of being
which can be grasped only by artistic
creativity. . . . One could speak of
expressive truth or untruth. But one should
instead speak of the authenticity of the
expressive form or of its unauthenticity.[93]

Taking this statement in conjunction with the preceding, we
can say that Tillich is aware that the application of the term
"true" to what is, like poetry, simply revelatory, may be misleading. Insights, poetry, revelatory utterances--none are matters of "information." They are not conceptual. They precede
the conceptual, in the way that power precedes rationality in
being itself.

But what about the conceptual? What is it? In what sense
does it have to do with truth? In what sense can we be said to
know something once we have conceptualized it? Poetry is revelatory but not conceptual. Tillich seems to suggest that one conceptualizes rather than simply expresses to the extent that one
gathers together insights or revelatory experiences.[94] A flash
of insight may make one aware of the beauty of a city, another
flash may make one see the ugliness of it. The poet might thus

---

[92] S.T., III, p. 399.

[93] Ibid., p. 64.

[94] I am using the words "insight" and "revelatory experience"
more or less interchangeably here, and I focus on the term
"insight" because it somehow seems more clear. Tillich himself
uses both terms and many others. Cf., for example, A History of
Christian Thought, p. 159, where Tillich says that "the church
cannot afford . . . to have here an insight and there an insight
which have nothing to do with each other or even contradict each
other." Here, too, we get the idea of truth involving both
insights and the relating of these insights, both power and form,
both experience and reason, or both ecstasy and structure.

write two poems; the philosopher or conceptual thinker will ask
how the same city can be both beautiful and ugly at the same time.
Is this a silly question? An answer to it may help in reconciling
a conflict between those who see the beauty of the city and thus
want to preserve it, and those who see the ugliness of it and
want to tear it down. On a more individual level, conceptualization might keep us from rejecting the "truth" (or authenticity)
of one of our own insights. Again and again we have seen the
value of consistency as lying, for Tillich, in its _integrating_
function. One way we seek personal and communal unity or integration is by conceptualizing, by grasping what can be grasped
in seemingly disparate insights and trying to reconcile them.

These insights, or presuppositions, are _given_, so to speak.
They "grasp" us. They constitute the way reality encounters us;
they constitute the way we see being itself. Insofar as we grasp
them, we conceptualize, relating them to one another or unifying
them. This unifying activity is what Tillich calls knowing; what
knowing aims at is what he calls truth.

To put things in the traditional jargon, Tillich has a
coherence theory of truth. Truth is what one would get if he
brought into relation all possible human insights without doing
an injustice to (or without rendering inauthentic) any of them.
We can _seek_ this aim, according to Tillich, and thus we can seek
truth. Truth, in this coherence sense, is obviously good, insofar as one thinks that integration of the self and the community
is good. Such truth is a function of love.

These suggestions are mere suggestions. Perhaps the most
that can be said for them is that they seem corroborated by what
Tillich says of and the way he practices ontology. Ontology is
the attempt to seek out our basic presuppositions, our insights,
the root-meanings of our basic concepts, in order to find their
unity, their rationality, or their consistency. The Hegelian
thrust behind Tillich's thought is clear enough, but one might
just as well call it a Platonic thrust. It involves the certainty,
which comes close to being certainty of the sort that definitions
have, that truth must be rational, and that it must be good. Why
must truth be rational? Because otherwise we would not call it
truth. Why must it be good (in the sense of promoting unity or
integration)? For the same reason.

In this sense a theology like Tillich's can claim to possess conceptual or theoretical truth. It can claim to do so
with respect to the contents of the Christian faith insofar as
it brings together the various revelatory insights or presuppo-

sitions expressed in the Scripture and tradition which constitute it as a religion. It can claim to do so with respect not
only to the particular contents of Christian experience but with
respect to the contents of human experience in general insofar as
it brings together the insights or presuppositions expressed in
universal human experience. Tillich tries to do both, because
he thinks religion and culture need each other.

The question, however, persists whether, apart from his
particular definition of truth, Tillich _really_ believes it is
possible to have _theoretical_ truth pure and simple. It would be
exasperating to hear Tillich respond by defining "theoretical"
in the sense according to which he can obviously reply affirma-
tively. We might wish to ask whether there is not some truth
about reality itself, _independent_ not only of the individual but
of human experience as such. Is there any way of going beyond
the mere unification of insights? Are these insights not, after
all, "mere" feelings? Does not Tillich in a sense go beyond
Schleiermacher only in a semantic way, by _ontologizing_ the
objects of feeling--i.e., by saying what Schleiermacher says
but not using terms like "feeling" but instead using terms like
"reality" or "being"? Is not Tillich simply exercising the old
theological ploy of conversion by definition--defining truth in
such a way that theology can have access to it?

What one wishes to ask Tillich is whether he thinks that
our insights, or any unification or structuring of them, correspond to reality as such, independent of man. That is, does
Tillich at least _say_ something about the so-called correspon-
dence view of truth? He does indeed. What he seems to believe
is, in fact, perhaps closer on the whole to Kant than to either
Hegel or Plato. Tillich thinks that reality or the truth about
reality is not exhausted by human experience and the structuring
of experience by reason. But this reality as such is something
we can know nothing of. It would be tantamount to knowing God
or being-itself directly, and for Tillich this is not possible.

> In history as well as in physics, in ethics as
> well as in medicine, the observer wants to regard
> the phenomenon as it "really" is. "Really"
> means independent of the observer. However,
> there is no such thing as independence from the
> observer. The observed changes in being observed.
> This has always been obvious in philosophy, the
> humanities, and history, but now it has also
> become so in biology, psychology, and physics.
> The result is not the "real" but encountered
> reality, and from the point of view of the
> meaning of absolute truth, encountered reality

is distorted reality.[95]

To put this in strictly theological terms, Tillich does not believe that we can have knowledge about God in himself, but only as he is for us. In _Philosophical_ _Interrogations_, Bertocci presses him on the question of how we can have cognitive certainty in religious experience. Tillich rejects the whole view of truth as an understanding of reality as such or of the real nature of God in his reply.

> The validity of the experience of faith (the state of being grasped by the spiritual Presence) is not diminished by the fact that our knowledge of the divine ground of our being refers to its relation to us, but not to its essence. The mystery of being itself is beyond the cognitive grasp of any finite being just because it transcends the subject-object scheme which of itself is the unquestioned presupposition of every "epistemic dualist." The attempt to do "cognitive justice to the Unconditioned" by dissolving its mystery would be the greatest cognitive injustice. The problem is not to find a more or less trustworthy cognitive approach to the divine, either by faith or by "the reasonable probability" of inference; the problem is one of participation itself. The cognitive expressions, based on the experience of participation, are of secondary importance and have no standing in themselves--a fact which makes it impossible to discover or to confirm them inferentially.[96]

The point is that the cognitive expressions of faith are not attempts to know God himself but are attempts to conceptualize particular experiences. These conceptualizations serve a purpose, but they "have no standing in themselves."

Tillich makes the same point in reply to another question by Bertocci regarding Tillich's concepts of before and after in the divine life and the question whether God is better after man's estrangement from him has been overcome. Tillich's answer, which he suggests is also his answer to Hartshorne and all those who accept a finite, humanly accessible God, is the following:

> Perhaps the basic difference is a different feeling about the unapproachable character of the divine mystery. I try, not always successfully, to avoid statements about the divine nature which transcend the merely relational, the "for us." A question such as: "Is God in _any_ valuational sense 'better' _because_ estrangement has been overcome?" would pro-

---

[95]_S.T._, III, p. 70.

[96]Rome, p. 388.

duce anxiety in me. . . . The philosophical problem is the concept of an "eternal
process." As always in the relation of the
eternal to the temporal, the only way of
speaking adequately is in boundary-line
fixations: Eternity is not timelessness;
and eternity is not endless temporality.
It lies, so to speak, between them, or,
more correctly, above them. For this "above,"
however, we have no possible concept; therefore the question of a "before" or "after"
in God cannot be answered.[97]

Thus we have to give two answers to the question whether
theology, by taking an ontological approach, can provide us with
truth. In the coherence sense of truth, it can; in the corres-
pondence sense, it cannot. And this is because ontology itself
has the same capacity and the same limitation. For our purposes,
the fundamental difference between ontology and theology can be
expressed as follows: whereas ontology attempts to express in
conceptual form the fundamental presuppositions of all men,
theology tries to express in conceptual form the fundamental
presuppositions of all Christian men.[98] And to the extent that
an ontological or philosophical or apologetic theology is possible, one is presupposing that these two tasks, ontology and theology, are in principle united.

E. Concluding Comments

Perhaps what is most surprising, to me at least, in this
whole study is the extent to which Tillich of all people, the
supposedly abstract ontological thinker who, again supposedly,
turns God into Being-itself and sacrifices the richness of Christian revelatory experience to the frozen, bloodless abstractions
of speculative philosophy, at least intends to be serving the
most practical Christian aim of all, the aim of love. I did not
expect to find this; I expected to be able to show that there is
a point at which Tillich just cannot claim to be serving the
church but is doing what simply gives him pleasure or what he
enjoys: seeking "truth" (in some bare, abstract sense). I
expected then to have to say that while the church might permit

---

[97]Ibid., p. 378.

[98]This greater narrowness of theology stems from an even
more fundamental difference between ontology and theology: that
ontology deals with "the structure of being in itself" while
theology deals with "the meaning of being for us" (S.T., I, p.
22). Note that Tillich does not say that ontology deals with
being in itself (which cannot be known) but with the structure
of being in itself, or being as it appears to human reason.

such activity among those within it who like to do this kind of
thing, it is necessary or valuable to the church no more than
(or just as much as) stamp-collecting, playing tennis, journalism,
or any other hobbies or "vocations."

But if Tillich is right that theology is through and through
aimed at serving the church, this would seem to have certain consequences for the way in which one approaches theological debates
with and examinations of other thinkers, living or dead. For I
have the impression that theological discussions are often somewhat deceptive: while claiming to be done in the service of the
church, it is not evident just how the resolution of a certain
problem could help anyone at all. Granted that through his pro-
vidential activity God might be working behind our backs to
justify or make just or make worthwhile such activity, there is
still no call to take this for granted. Theological thinking
might profit from examining more carefully what is the point of
such thinking about each particular problem under discussion.
Indeed, the theologian might even see himself called to ask such
a question. And perhaps one reason why theological thinking
today seems either to have power but no clear aim or else to have
clear aim but be simply barren is that theologians are hardly
aware what they are supposed to be doing or why they are supposed
to be doing it.

It is easy enough to say that theology serves the church; it
is more difficult to show how it serves the church. This showing
how, if it is to be worthwhile, cannot involve vague generalities,
but must rather consist of an effort again and again to reflect
upon one's particular arguments, rhetoric, persuasive definitions,
interpretations, and all one's indications of rational or irrational approval or disapproval, reflecting upon them in the light
of the questions: what difference does it make, and particularly,
does it make the difference I intend it to make? And if it does
not, perhaps it would be good either to try very hard to rectify
things or, if one does not see the way to do that, to simply be
quiet for awhile.

We have tried in this study to find Tillich's most fundamental, or most defensible, intent, not to criticize that intent
or even to ask whether Tillich successfully carries it out. In
particular, we have wanted to find out what Tillich is trying to
do when he argues; we have not evaluated the arguments themselves
because we wanted to see the point of arguing, and of evaluating
arguments, in the first place. And if we accept Tillich's view
that as we approach the essential meaning or intent of a thinker

we approach a level at which he is united with other thinkers, then this work should have bearing not only on the question of the purpose of his philosophy and theology but also on the question of the purpose of philosophy and theology in general. It is my conviction that only as we become clear about this purpose can our philosophical and theological arguments help make the world better instead of even more confused. Perhaps a summary paragraph can remind us of the point to which we have been led.

For Tillich the fundamental task of ontology or philosophy is to seek out the common ground which is presupposed in our encounter with reality. And the fundamental task of apologetic or philosophical theology is much the same. This <u>cognitive</u> search for the common ground is one of the ways of love, of love as both philosophical <u>eros</u> and religious <u>agape</u>: we <u>recognize</u> that we have been given (or that there is within us) both the need and the command, and through the New Being the power, to be reconciled to one another, to find the ground which is common to ourselves and other men. It is no idle play on words but a clarification of Tillich's concept of the divine to note that this search for the common ground can be expressed as the search for the <u>common ground of our being</u>; it is the search for being-itself, or God.

Bibliography

Brown, D. Mackenzie (ed.) Ultimate Concern: Tillich in Dialogue. New York: Harper and Row, 1965.

Kegley, Charles W., and Bretall, Robert W. (eds.) The Theology of Paul Tillich. New York: The Macmillan Company, 1956.

Rome, Sidney, and Rome, Beatrice (eds.) Philosophical Interrogations. New York: Holt, Rinehart and Winston, 1964.

Tillich, Paul. Biblical Religion and the Search for Ultimate Reality. Chicago: The University of Chicago Press, 1955.

_____. The Courage to Be. New Haven; Yale University Press, 1952.

_____. Dynamics of Faith. New York: Harper and Brothers, 1957.

_____. The Future of Religions. Edited by Jerald C. Brauer. New York: Harper and Row, 1966.

_____. A History of Christian Thought. Edited by Carl E. Braaten. New York: Harper and Row, 1968.

_____. Love, Power, and Justice: Ontological Analyses and Ethical Applications. New York: Oxford University Press, 1954.

_____. Perspectives on Nineteenth and Twentieth Century Protestant Theology. Edited by Carl E. Braaten. New York: Harper and Row, 1967.

_____. The Protestant Era. Translated by James Luther Adams. Abridged edition. Chicago: The University of Chicago Press, 1957.

_____. Systematic Theology. 3 volumes. Chicago: The University of Chicago Press, 1951-1963.

_____. Das System der Wissenschaften nach Gegenstanden und Methoden. Gottingen: Vandenhoeck and Ruprecht, 1923.

_____. Theology of Culture. Edited by Robert C. Kimball. London: Oxford University Press, 1959.